THE COURAGE TO CHANGE

THE COURAGE TO CHANGE

SAYING GOODBYE TO GOOD ENOUGH
AND EMBRACING THE PROMISE OF
WHAT CAN BE

JOYCE MEYER

NEW YORK · NASHVILLE

FaithWords
Hachette Book Group
1290 Avenue of the Americas, New York, NY 10104
faithwords.com
@FaithWords / @FaithWordsBooks

First Edition: May 2025

FaithWords is a division of Hachette Book Group, Inc. The FaithWords name and
logo are registered trademarks of Hachette Book Group, Inc.

The publisher is not responsible for websites (or their content)
that are not owned by the publisher.

The Hachette Speakers Bureau provides a wide range of authors for speaking
events. To find out more, go to hachettespeakersbureau.com or email
HachetteSpeakers@hbgusa.com.

FaithWords books may be purchased in bulk for business, educational, or
promotional use. For information, please contact your local bookseller or the
Hachette Book Group Special Markets Department at special.markets@hbgusa.com.

Library of Congress Cataloging-in-Publication Data
Names: Meyer, Joyce, 1943- author.
Title: The courage to change : saying goodbye to good enough and embracing the
promise of what can be / Joyce Meyer.
Description: First edition. | New York : Faith Words, 2025.
Identifiers: LCCN 2024054885 | ISBN 9781546005810 (hardcover) | ISBN
9781546005834 (ebook)
Subjects: LCSH: Change (Psychology)—Religious aspects—Christianity. | Christian life.
Classification: LCC BV4599.5.C44 M485 2025 | DDC 248.4—dc23/eng/20250109
LC record available at https://lccn.loc.gov/2024054885

ISBNs: 978-1-5460-0581-0 (hardcover), 978-1-5460-0921-4 (large type),
978-1-5460-0583-4 (ebook)

Printed in the United States of America

LSC-C

Printing 1, 2025

CONTENTS

Introduction   vii

Part 1: Walking with God through Life's Changes   1

Chapter 1   The Greatest Change of All   3
Chapter 2   God Changes People's Lives   15

Part 2: How Your Mind Affects Change   27

Chapter 3   Change Your Mind about Change   29
Chapter 4   The Key to Transformation   41
Chapter 5   Adjust Your Attitude   53
Chapter 6   Stay at Peace   65

Part 3: Managing Change Well   77

Chapter 7   Little by Little   79
Chapter 8   Understand That Change Is a Process   93
Chapter 9   How to Handle the Changes in
             Your Life, Part 1   107
Chapter 10 How to Handle the Changes in
             Your Life, Part 2   119

Chapter 11 Control Your Emotions   131
Chapter 12 Let Go and Let God   143

Part 4: Let Change Move You Forward   153

Chapter 13 Perfection Is Impossible   155
Chapter 14 Possessing Your Inheritance   167
Chapter 15 The Courage to Change   179

Conclusion   193

INTRODUCTION

Change happens to everyone, and it's happening all the time, all around us. Sometimes I feel the world is changing faster than some people can keep up with it. When I think about the way life was in the United States when I was growing up in the 1940s and '50s, the changes I have witnessed are mind-boggling. Of course, technology has impacted the world and precipitated changes in ways previous generations could not have imagined. This has resulted in new industries, new ways of communication, and new ways of working. In addition, values and priorities have changed. Social structures have changed, and even nations have changed. There are countries on the map today that didn't exist even thirty years ago.

We change our minds about how we think about things, we go through life transitions, and our friends change. We may have had someone in our life for many years, and for a variety of reasons they are no longer present. They may have died, moved, or simply changed what they are doing, and their time is occupied with that instead of with us.

Change is all around us, happening every day, in big and small ways. People's tastes and expectations change.

Our relationships change, our jobs change, our finances change. Our children grow up and leave the nest. Our bodies change as we get older. If we take good care of ourselves, we can slow down the process of aging, but no one looks at eighty the way they did at twenty. I speak from experience. Society changes, styles change, and what people value changes.

I've experienced quite a few changes in my own life and ministry recently. Our ministry employs several hundred people, and what employees expect now is very different from what they expected thirty-five years ago. Not all those changes have been easy for me, but sometimes we must change, whether we want to or not. For example, working from home is popular today, and computers make it possible for people to work from almost anywhere, at any time. Even though I am more accustomed to an 8 a.m. to 5 p.m. workday, I have had to change my mind.

We are all products of the era in which we grew up, and we usually like things the way they were. But if we are not willing to change, we will probably get left behind while everyone else moves on. We must remember that just because something was right for 1980 doesn't mean it is right for 2025 or 2030. I know people who stubbornly cling to "the good ol' days," and they are not effective in the present.

Even though everything around us shakes and changes, only God never changes (Malachi 3:6). God's Word doesn't change (Isaiah 40:8), and it should dictate our standard and style of living. Everyone and everything else is subject to change. Because God always remains the same and His Word is always true and powerful, we can have the courage to change.

About twenty years ago, our conference attendance was declining. As I looked around at the crowds, I realized that the people there were about the same age I was. This wasn't a good sign because it meant I wasn't reaching younger people. Our son Daniel, who was about twenty years old at the time, had recently come to work for us in a position of authority and suggested many changes that I resisted at first. He recommended having younger bands lead worship, updating the way I dressed, and modernizing the look of our platform. He also advised changing our monthly magazine and even redecorating some of our office space.

At first, I felt insulted by my son's ideas, as though he was saying I had not done a good job. But he helped me understand that this wasn't the case. I had taken the ministry to the point where it was, but the time had come when I needed input from people who were younger than I was.

One day, in a meeting, the discussion got a bit heated. I finally said, "Dan, everyone here agrees with me." He replied, "Of course they do. They're all the same age you are." He was right, and we have let him make the changes he suggested. Even though I didn't particularly like all of them, I must admit that he was correct, and our ministry has grown. Now when I look at the crowds at our conferences, I see people of all ages, from all walks of life, not just people of my generation. The growth our ministry has experienced has enabled us to help more people. Had I refused to change because of stubborn pride, I might not even have a ministry now.

I hope the story about our ministry helps you realize how important it is to be willing to be open to change. Perhaps you are facing some changes right now and are struggling with them, or perhaps you need to make some changes and are afraid to do so. I know that change requires courage, but I also know that leaving behind an old season and embracing the new experiences God has for you will be worth it through any anxiety or fear. Don't ever be afraid to give up the good to go for the great! We had a good ministry, but now it is better than ever.

> *Don't be afraid to give up the good for the great.*

We are facing more changes right now and are still in the process of deciding what they should be. But I know that when God closes one door, He always opens another. Don't miss what God wants to do in your life now because you are clinging to the past. Have the courage to change.

PART 1

Walking with God through Life's Changes

CHAPTER 1

The Greatest Change of All

Therefore if any person is [ingrafted] in Christ (the Messiah) he is a new creation (a new creature altogether); the old [previous moral and spiritual condition] has passed away. Behold, the fresh and new has come!

2 Corinthians 5:17

I believe the greatest change of all and the greatest miracle we witness is how God changes people. This chapter's opening scripture says that when we are in Christ, we become new creatures altogether. We are changed on the inside, and we need to learn to live "inside out." When we surrender our lives to Jesus and receive Him as Lord and Savior, I like to say that we become new spiritual clay. The Holy Spirit begins the process of molding us into the image of Jesus Christ (Romans 8:29). God comes to live in us and the seed (essence) of all we need to develop His character is present in us. It simply needs to be watered with God's Word and worked out in our behavior as the Holy Spirit reveals truth to us and teaches us how to love. Becoming new is a difficult journey, but it is also very exciting. The more we learn to surrender to the Holy Spirit and His work in our lives, the easier the process of transformation is.

I have learned this lesson firsthand. I have needed many changes in my life over the years, and God has been faithful in bringing them about in His timing and in His ways. He has walked me through each one, and they have all been positive. I needed the changes desperately, and I do not think they would have happened apart from a relationship with God.

My Awakening

I had a tormented childhood, and by the time I began to walk with God, I needed deep healing in my soul and many changes in my thinking and behavior. When I came to realize through God's Word that Satan had robbed me of peace, joy, righteousness, dignity, and confidence, and that he had stolen my childhood through abuse, I became furious and wanted to lash out at everyone. I felt that something was owed to me, but I kept trying to collect from the wrong people.

When I realized how much the devil had stolen from me because my father sexually abused me, I felt cheated. Even more frustrating, I realized I had wasted a lot of years in negative mindsets and emotions and could never get those years back. I did not want to continue repeating the same cycle of bad attitudes, so I decided something needed to change.

You can't change your history, but you can change your destiny.

It was too late to change the circumstances that made me unhappy, but over time, I learned many lessons that finally got me on the right path. I learned that I couldn't change my history, but I could change my destiny. I learned that even though I didn't have a good beginning, I could have a good ending. I learned that God would repay me for my former shame (Isaiah 61:7). I learned that we only overcome evil with good (Romans 12:21). And I learned a very important lesson: Many of the changes I needed depended on forgiving the people who had hurt me. As long as we remain bitter and unforgiving, we cannot make any forward progress in life. In fact, I believe it is so vital that I have written an entire section on it in chapter 12, "Let Go and Let God."

I had to change my thinking to change my future, and it certainly wasn't easy. None of the changes were easy, but they were necessary if I didn't want to perpetuate the miserable existence I had been living. Trouble is a promise, but misery is an option.

> Trouble is a promise, but misery is an option.

God's Word says that we are to forget the former things and not dwell on the past because He is doing a new thing and doesn't want us to miss it (Isaiah 43:18–19).

Over a period of years of step-by-step obedience to God, my life changed, and I am no longer angry, resentful, or even sorry about what happened to me during my childhood, because I know God is working it out for good.

The First Step toward Change

Facing the truth about ourselves and our current behavior is the first step toward change. We cannot change unless we know we need to. This was true for me, and it's true for you. Jesus says that if we continue in His Word, we will know the truth and the truth

> You cannot change unless you know you need to.

will set us free (John 8:31–32). The Holy Spirit is the Spirit of Truth (John 14:17), and Jesus says, "I am the Way and the Truth and the Life" (John 14:6). Jesus is also the Word who became flesh and came to dwell among us (John 1:14). There is no possibility of knowing truth without knowing Jesus and allowing His Spirit to work in your life.

The Old Testament prophet Jeremiah writes, "The heart is deceitful above all things" (Jeremiah 17:9 NIV). It is very easy to deceive ourselves about ourselves, but we cannot do anything about something that we don't know exists. When God reveals to us something that needs to be corrected, it is a manifestation of His love. I'm grateful that God loves me too much to leave me the way I am.

Our world today is so confusing that many people are asking "What is truth?" They often say truth is relative, meaning that it must be considered or judged alongside other things. Most of the time today, people think of truth as whatever each person wants to make it in their life. I believe this is a big reason the world is in the condition it is in. Jesus doesn't say He is "a truth"; He says He is "the Truth." Anyone who follows His guidelines for life knows that following them is the only way to live that produces true peace, joy, and right relationship with God.

When a person is born again (receives Jesus as Lord and Savior) and begins to study or hear His Word, that person will be convicted of sin and want to change. They will want their behavior to align with God's Word. The best way to accomplish this is to first admit sin, then repent of it, receive God's forgiveness, and be willing to turn away from the sin. Then, instead of simply "trying" to change, they need to ask God to help them. They may fall back into old habits several times before new habits are firmly established. If you do this and find yourself reverting to old ways, do not feel condemned. Simply start over. The righteous person falls seven times and gets up again (Proverbs 24:16).

Conviction (recognizing a need to change) is from God, but condemnation is from the devil. Condemnation hinders spiritual growth and is not helpful in any way. I wasted at least twenty-five years of my relationship with God

> Conviction is from God; condemnation is from the devil.

feeling guilty and condemned and "trying" hard to change before I realized that only God could change me and that I needed to ask Him to do it. He changes us as we study His Word, pray, and spend time with Him. He often shows us things we can do, and when He does, we should do them. But if what we do isn't Spirit-led, it is useless. Success in any area is not by might nor by power, but by the Holy Spirit (Zechariah 4:6).

The apostle Paul reveals a personal dilemma in Romans 7:15–8:2. The process he went through is no different from what you and I go through as we seek to be like Jesus. He starts by saying that he can't seem to do what he wants to do, and he finds himself doing what he doesn't want to do. Take the time to read about this below in the Message translation, because this paraphrase makes the passage very clear:

> What I don't understand about myself is that I decide one way, but then I act another, doing things I absolutely despise. So if I can't be trusted to figure out what is best for myself and then do it, it becomes obvious that God's command is necessary. But I need something *more*! For if I know the law but still can't keep it, and if the power of sin within me keeps sabotaging my best intentions, I obviously need help! I realize that I don't have what it takes. I can will it, but I can't *do* it. I decide to do good, but I don't *really* do it; I decide not to do bad, but then I do it anyway. My decisions, such as they are, don't result in actions. Something has gone wrong deep within me and gets the better of me every time. It happens so regularly that it's predictable. The moment I decide to do good, sin is there to trip me up. I truly delight in God's commands, but it's pretty obvious that not all of me joins in that delight. Parts of me covertly rebel, and just when I least expect it, they take charge. I've tried everything and nothing helps. I'm at the end of my rope. Is there no one who can do anything for me? Isn't that the real question? The answer,

thank God, is that Jesus Christ can and does.
He acted to set things right in this life of contra-
dictions where I want to serve God with all my
heart and mind, but am pulled by the influence
of sin to do something totally different.

Romans 7:15–25 MSG

Only God can deliver us, and only He can change us. As
we wait on Him to do so, we are not to be condemned but to
be full of faith and very thankful that God has delivered us.
We need to claim the victory God has given us while it is
becoming a reality in our lives. For example, let's say a person who is impatient realizes it is not God's will for them
to be impatient, so they repent and ask God to help them
be patient. Each time they display impatience, they may
say "I'm so impatient." But what they should say is "God
is working patience in me and changing me little by little."

If you have never been taught this or heard anything like
this, it may seem odd to you. But Romans 4:17 says that we
serve a God who "calls those things which do not exist
as though they did" (NKJV). We should speak according to
who we are "in Christ," meaning spiritually, not according
to how we currently behave. To speak by faith is not to
tell a lie; it is stating what is yours spiritually—what you
are growing into in Christ—as a child of God. Our words
are powerful, and if I keep hearing "I'm so impatient," I
will continue to be impatient. But if I hear "In Christ, I am
patient," then I will eventually produce what I believe.

The best way to deal with the changes in your life is to face them with God and believe what He says in His Word. He loves you and has a wonderful plan for your life. You can trust that God knows what He is doing in your life and that it will work out for your good (Romans 8:28). Change often hurts, but in the end, it frees us and makes us glad.

Questions

1. How has God changed you?

   _____

   _____

   _____

2. What does the fact that you cannot change your history but you can change your destiny mean to you?

   _____

   _____

   _____

3. What change would you like to see in your life in order to give up the good and go for the great?

   _____

   _____

   _____

4. What is the first step you can take to begin to move your life from good to great?

_____

_____

_____

5. Why is it important to speak faith-filled words as you are waiting on God to bring about a complete change in your life?

_____

_____

_____

CHAPTER 2

God Changes People's Lives

"For I know the plans I have for you," declares the Lord, "plans to prosper you and not to harm you, plans to give you hope and a future."

Jeremiah 29:11 NIV

Contrary to what some people think, the people we read about in the Bible were ordinary people just like you and me. Many of them committed gross sins, yet through repentance and the mercy of God, they went on to overcome their past and fulfill God's purposes for their lives. Each of the people mentioned in this chapter had a heart for God, and even though they didn't do everything right, God intervened in their circumstances and changed their lives.

Jacob Was Determined to Meet with God—and It Changed Everything

Jacob, one of the three patriarchs, made many mistakes early in his life. He cheated, swindled, and deceived people. Jacob and his brother, Esau, were twins. Of the two, Esau was born first, which automatically gave him the birthright, the rights and privileges of the firstborn son, including inheriting his father's authority and a double portion of his possessions.

Jacob took advantage of Esau at a time when Esau was hungry. He talked Esau into selling him his birthright for a bowl of stew (Genesis 25:29–34). I see two problems with this: Jacob was wrong to take advantage of Esau when he was weak, and Esau was also wrong because he disrespected his birthright to the point of being willing to sell it for something to eat. When Jacob and Esau's father, Isaac, was old and approaching death, his eyesight was dim. He called for Esau so he could give him his blessing. But Rebekah, Isaac's wife and the boys' mother, convinced Jacob to deceive his father. He did this by pretending to be Esau and taking the blessing for himself (Genesis 27:1–29).

Once the blessing had been given, even though Isaac realized he had given it to Jacob instead of Esau, he could not take it back (Genesis 27:30–40). Esau, of course, became angry about this and planned to kill Jacob, so Rebekah feared for her younger son's life (Genesis 27:41–42). She told him to go live with her brother Laban in Haran until Esau calmed down (Genesis 27:43–45). Jacob ended up staying in Haran for twenty years and building a family there (Genesis 31:38) until he grew tired of living with Laban and dealing with his lying and cheating (Genesis 30:25–26; 31:7). When God saw how Laban mistreated Jacob, something needed to change. God told Jacob to return to his homeland (Genesis 31:3, 12–13). Jacob walked away from everything, determined that he would meet with God and follow Him from that point on.

One night, Jacob got up and "took his two wives, his two women servants, and his eleven sons and passed over the ford [of the] Jabbok" (Genesis 32:22), a tributary of the Jordan River. He also sent over all that he had. When he was left alone, "a Man wrestled with him until daybreak" (Genesis 32:24).

The Man Jacob wrestled with was the Angel of the Lord.

As they wrestled, Jacob refused to give up. When the Man realized Jacob was not letting Him win, He touched the hollow of Jacob's thigh, putting it out of joint as they struggled (Genesis 32:25).

The Man then said, "Let Me go, for day is breaking," but Jacob said, "I will not let You go unless You declare a blessing on me" (Genesis 32:26). I see this as a powerful picture of Jacob's determination to turn his life around.

In response to Jacob's refusal to let the Man go unless He blessed him, the Man asked Jacob, "What is your name?" Jacob replied, "Jacob [supplanter, schemer, trickster, swindler]!" (Genesis 32:27). He realized he had been strong-willed and self-sufficient, and the limp that resulted from having his thigh out of joint reminded him for the rest of his life of the result of self-will.

Just as Jacob demonstrated humility when he admitted the truth about himself, we must face the truth about ourselves and our behavior if we want to make progress in our lives. If we are deceived about who we are and how we act, we will not be open to making the changes God wants us to make because we will not realize we need them.

> Face the truth about yourself if you want to make progress in your life.

The Man (remember, this was the Angel of the Lord) told Jacob he would no longer be called Jacob, meaning "supplanter," but he would be called "Israel [contender with God]" (v. 28). This was because he had contended with and now had power with God and with people because he

prevailed. This shows me that God likes it when we refuse
to give up. Anyone can turn their life

> You can turn
> your life around
> with God's help.

around with God's help, no matter how
bad they have been in the past, if they
really want to.

Even though Jacob's early life was characterized by
wrongdoing, through repentance and a refusal to give up,
God blessed him. He walked with a limp the remainder
of his life, but he and Esau eventually reconciled (Genesis
33:3–4), and they had both experienced God's blessings.

This story helps us understand how merciful God is and
that if we are willing to change, we can be blessed in the
future, no matter what our past has been.

A Dramatic Change in Paul's Life

One of the Bible's most remarkable stories of transformation occurs in the life of the apostle Paul (formerly known
as Saul). He was born into a Jewish family and educated by
one of the esteemed rabbis of his day. He became a Pharisee
and ended up persecuting followers of Jesus. Saul not only
consented to Stephen's stoning, but the amplification says,
"he was pleased and entirely approving" of it (Acts 8:1).

According to Acts 8:3, "Saul shamefully treated and laid
waste the church continuously [with cruelty and violence];
and entering house after house, he dragged out men and
women and committed them to prison." One day, while
Saul was still filled with evil desires, he was traveling on

the road to Damascus when he was surrounded by a bright light, and he fell to the ground. Jesus called out to him, asking him why he was persecuting Him. Saul recognized the Lord was speaking to him and asked, "What do you want me to do?" When Saul got up and opened his eyes, he was blind. He was given instructions to go to a certain house where a man would be ready to minister to him (Acts 9:1–11).

Three days later, Saul's sight was restored, and he was filled with the Holy Spirit (Acts 9:17–18). This changed him *completely*. He ended up being one of the greatest apostles in Christian history and wrote a large part of the New Testament. He went from being a persecutor of Christians to becoming a world-changer for the cause of Christ.

Paul brought the message of salvation by grace through faith in Christ, and no one could have done it better because he experienced God's grace himself.

Peter Becomes Bold

Peter, one of Jesus' twelve disciples, was known for being passionate, impetuous, and having a temper. At times, he was fiercely loyal to Jesus, but one night he totally denied even knowing Christ three times (Luke 22:54–61). Afterward, he felt bitter remorse for having done it (Luke 22:62). Jesus forgave him, and God used him mightily (John 21:15–19). Shortly after he denied Christ, Peter was filled with the Holy Spirit (endued with power that makes a person bold and courageous), and he preached so boldly in Jerusalem that three thousand souls were baptized and added to the church in one day (Acts 2:14–41).

Peter went on to have a powerful ministry and to write two epistles in the New Testament—1 Peter and 2 Peter. It is amazing how a touch from God can change our lives forever. I urge you to pray regularly to stay filled with the Holy Spirit, as Peter was. When we are filled with the Holy Spirit, we sense His leadership and guidance in every area of our lives. This is especially helpful as we navigate the new experiences we face when dealing with change.

David Changes Direction—Twice

David, the king of Israel, had been walking closely with God all his life. Then one day, he succumbed to temptation and sinned against God when he saw his neighbor Bathsheba bathing and lusted after her. He had intercourse with her, even though they were both married to other people (2 Samuel 11:2–4). When she became pregnant, he had her husband killed in battle and took her as his wife (2 Samuel 11:5, 14–17, 27). The child she conceived died at birth, and David was never without war after that (2 Samuel 12:10–18). But God did forgive him, and he remained king (2 Samuel 12:13).

God referred to David as a man after his own heart (Acts 13:22). Here we see a man who had a heart for God and a close relationship with Him commit a terrible sin. This is a good example that shows us the weakness of human flesh. David had a weakness, but he was not wicked.

The story of David's sin with Bathsheba begins when other kings went to war and David stayed home (2 Samuel 11:1). He sent Joab, the commander of his army, and the entire Israelite army to war, but he stayed in his palace, away from the battle. This was when he saw Bathsheba bathing on her rooftop and was overcome with temptation (2 Samuel 11:2). Perhaps, had David been where he should have been—at the head of his army with the rest of the kings—he would not have sinned with Bathsheba.

There are times in life when we, like David, are in places we should not be, and Satan uses those circumstances to draw us into temptation.

David came to a place of deep sorrow and repentance for his actions, and his heart turned back to God. His prayer is recorded in Psalm 51. God forgave him, of course, and went on to use him powerfully as a leader of His people. God's mercy is truly amazing.

Change Is a Privilege and a Gift

Things that don't change eventually die. The ability to change is one of the greatest privileges we have as human beings, and it is a gift from God. It is part of the way He matures us, brings us fulfillment in life, and moves us forward into His unfolding plans for us. I encourage you to believe that change can happen in your life. Based on Matthew 19:26, which says that all things are possible with God, begin to speak aloud "I can change" or "Things in my life can change." As they do change, remember that, as a believer, you don't walk alone through the changes you face. The Holy Spirit is leading you along a path of wonderful growth and transformation.

> *Your ability to change is a gift from God.*

We all have loved ones we are concerned about because they are not walking with God, but we should not think or say that they will never change. God changed Saul, who became Paul, in an instant, and one touch from God can change the people you love too.

Questions

1. What major changes has God brought about in your life?

   _____

   _____

   _____

2. In what ways can you relate to the following people in whose lives God intervened?
   - Jacob
   - Paul

- Peter
- David

_____

_____

_____

3. Why can change be considered "a privilege and a gift"?

_____

_____

_____

4. How does Matthew 19:26 encourage you to believe that change can happen in your life?

_____

_____

_____

5. Are you praying for your loved ones who do not know Him? Who are you praying for specifically?

_____

_____

_____

PART 2

How Your Mind Affects Change

CHAPTER 3

Change Your Mind about Change

Those who cannot change their minds cannot change anything.

George Bernard Shaw[1]

Many people are dealing with change. Either they want something to change but are afraid of change, or something is changing when they don't want it to, so they resist it. But all of us can set our minds to manage change well. Change is more difficult when it comes into our lives unexpectedly or when we are not the ones who planned it than when we do expect it or plan it. Sometimes other people choose to change, and that forces a change on us. Not many of us like to have things forced on us. But when they are, we can choose whether we will adjust or be left out of the new situation.

I noted in chapter 1 that the first step in the process of change is to be willing to let God change us. Another important step is to change our minds about change. Our minds are powerful. The thoughts we think control most aspects of our words, our behavior, and our feelings. Our minds can help us as we make the changes we need to make or as we deal with the ones that feel forced on us. Change is not always negative; many times, it is positive, and it is necessary for growth and progress. I believe this saying to be true: "Only a fool thinks he can always do what he has always done."

Sometimes you and I make changes and don't mind them because we are the ones who initiate them. But what happens when someone else changes something and the change affects you and you don't like it? For example, let's suppose you work at a place that provides insurance for you, and they change insurance companies. If you prefer the previous insurance company, you might be upset or even angry, but your emotions probably won't cause your employer to reconsider. If you want peace, you have to change your mind about the new company and begin to think, *This will work out well; I just need to get used to it*, or *This is the way it is, so there's no point in being upset about it.* You can also try being thankful that your company offers any insurance at all because millions of people don't have it through their jobs.

When we don't like a change, we tend to judge the people who made that change. But we should realize that they

> Submit to changes with a good attitude.

have perspectives and responsibilities we don't have and trust that they have good reasons for making the changes they make.

Much of our upset over change comes from the fact that we resist it, and we can solve that by submitting to changes with a good attitude. I believe God has created us with a need to change as time passes. We get bored with the same things over and over for years on end, and we may say, "Something needs to change," without realizing the importance of doing our part to initiate change, if needed, and the importance of changing any negative mindsets we have toward change.

Following Christ Involves Change

Becoming a Christian is all about change. For example, as we walk with God over time:

- We become positive instead of negative.
- We believe God's Word instead of doubting.
- We live by faith instead of according to our feelings.
- We think of others instead of being selfish and self-centered.
- We become generous and giving instead of holding on to things for ourselves and being selfish.
- We forgive instead of holding grudges.
- We become kind instead of cruel.
- We seek to do what God wants us to do instead of what we want to do.
- We lean on God's strength instead of relying on our human abilities.
- We learn to trust God instead of getting upset when things happen that we don't like.

These are just a few changes we will make as we grow in our relationship with God. I think I can safely say that the more we are able to embrace change, the happier we will be as Christians, because following Jesus involves change. We can trust Him as we go through changes, because He is always leading us into a better life.

The Good Life

*For we are God's [own] handiwork (His workman-
ship), recreated in Christ Jesus, [born anew] that
we may do those good works which God predestined
(planned beforehand) for us [taking paths which
He prepared ahead of time], that we should walk in
them [living the good life which He prearranged and
made ready for us to live].*

Ephesians 2:10

God has already prepared a good life for each of us
(Ephesians 2:10), and all we need to do is walk the path
that leads us to it. This sounds simple enough, so why
do we often live less-than lives when such good ones are
available? We do this because of the way we think. Proverbs 23:7 says, "For as he thinks in his heart, so is he." I
like to communicate this idea this way: "Where the mind
goes, the man follows." If my thoughts are filled with fear
and dread, how can I walk in faith? And faith is necessary
for us to enjoy the life Jesus has provided. Jesus says that
if we only believe (meaning to have faith), we will see the
glory (goodness) of God (John 11:40). This tells me that if
we don't believe, we won't see the goodness of God. This
involves more than simply believing that Jesus died for us
and that through faith in Him our sins are forgiven. It also

requires believing everything else He says in His Word. It requires trusting when we don't understand.

I may sincerely believe that Jesus died, paid for my sin, was buried, and rose from the grave, but not believe the other promises in His Word. In fact, I may not even be aware of how important it is to believe them. I lived this way prior to learning the importance of knowing God's Word and having my mind renewed accordingly. Once I learned how vital it is to believe all God's promises and began to do it, my life changed dramatically. I believe the same will happen to you as your mind is renewed and as you personally believe the promises God gives us in His Word. Trusting God leads us into His rest, and that is a wonderful place to be.

How Do You Think?

Do your thoughts agree with God's Word (His thoughts), or are they more in line with the world's thinking? You see, the world thinks we should believe what we see and feel above all else, but God tells us to believe what He promises no matter what we see or think at the moment. We must learn to see with the eyes of faith. Faith "is the assurance (the confirmation, the title deed) of the things [we] hope for, being the proof of things [we] do not see *and* the conviction of their reality [faith perceiving as real fact what is not revealed to the senses]" (Hebrews 11:1). We are more than conquerors according to

> *Always believe what God promises.*

God's Word (Romans 8:37), and I think this means we can be assured we will have victory over a problem before we even have the problem.

In 2023, I had nerve damage in my right leg and couldn't use it until it healed. During that time, I broke my left leg, so I couldn't use that leg either. I couldn't walk at all for about two months, was in the hospital twice, and was also in a rehabilitation hospital for twenty-four days. I was unable to do my conferences or much of anything else. For two months, I basically went three places: the bed, the recliner, and the bathroom. Simply moving from one of those places to the other was very difficult. But I can say that the entire time, from the very beginning, I believed I would get completely well and that God would take care of everything. He did. I did get well and am doing fine.

We all face trials in life, and they are usually unexpected. What we believe during those trials may affect our level of joy as we go through them and influence how long they will last and what the outcome will be. What you believe (think) is probably more important than you even realize.

If we want to change, the Bible tells us that we must be constantly renewed in the spirit of our mind "having a fresh mental and spiritual attitude" (Ephesians 4:23). If you want something to change, your thinking must change first.

When David faced Goliath, I don't think he stood before him thinking, *Oh, he is so much bigger than I am. He is a trained soldier, and I am a shepherd. Everyone has told me*

I can't do this, and if I try, I will probably fail. Instead, I believe David thought about the victories God had given him in the past when he killed a lion and a bear (1 Samuel 17:36). I'm sure he thought about God and believed God would give him victory if he stepped out in faith instead of cowering in fear.

When David saw Goliath and observed how the soldiers feared him, he said, "Who is this uncircumcised Philistine that he should defy the armies of the living God?" (1 Samuel 17:26). David believed he could conquer Goliath because He knew that God was with him. He did indeed conquer him, with a slingshot and a smooth stone (1 Samuel 17:40, 49). David believed what didn't make sense to the natural mind. He had faith and believed that God is faithful and would give him victory. He believed he had the victory before the battle began. He was more than a conqueror (Romans 8:37).

The Bible includes many accounts of people who believed in God's faithfulness in the face of seemingly impossible circumstances. Their faith defeated their circumstances.

- Joseph believed that God could work something good out of an evil, unjust, and painful situation (Genesis 37–50).
- Daniel believed he would not be left alone in the lions' den (Daniel 6:10–24).
- A woman who was sick for twelve years believed she could be healed, and while trying to get to Jesus, she

kept thinking and saying, "If I just touch his clothes, I will be healed." (Mark 5:28 NIV).

• Sarah believed she would have a child, even though she was far beyond childbearing age (Hebrews 11:11).

In the Old Testament book of Nehemiah, we read that Jerusalem was in a state of ruin after the Babylonian exile. The walls of the city had been torn down, so the people had no protection from their enemies. Nehemiah was living in Persia at the time, but he heard about the devastation of Jerusalem and believed the walls could be rebuilt (Nehemiah 1:3; 2:17–18). Through great perseverance, he and a group of men did rebuild them (Nehemiah 6:15). We often look at the people in the Bible as though they were superhuman beings, but they were ordinary people just like you and me, and they chose to believe God over their circumstances.

The people I have mentioned in this section and many other people whose stories are recorded in the Bible believed things that seemed impossible. Their thoughts agreed with God's Word. And God's Word tells us that "all things are possible with God" (Matthew 19:26); therefore, we should not allow ourselves to meditate on thoughts that say, "That's impossible." According to Philippians 4:13, when we are in Christ, we can do all things through Him because He gives us strength. Anything and anyone can change.

> *Do not allow yourself to think "That's impossible."*

Change your thinking to agree with God's thinking (His Word) if you want to live in and enjoy His good plan for your life and to navigate the changes He brings into your life as you continue to fulfill His purposes.

Questions

1. Why is it important to "change your mind" about change?

_____

_____

_____

2. When have you initiated a positive change in your life and been happy with the result?

_____

_____

_____

3. When has someone else forced change on you, and how did that affect you?

_____

_____

_____

4. Which of these changes are you experiencing as you
   follow Christ?
   • becoming positive instead of negative
   • believing God's Word instead of doubting
   • living by faith instead of according to your feelings
   • thinking of others instead of being selfish and
     self-centered
   • becoming generous and giving instead of holding on
     to things for yourself and being selfish
   • forgiving instead of holding grudges
   • becoming kind instead of cruel
   • seeking to do what God wants you to do instead of
     what you want to do
   • leaning on God's strength instead of relying on your
     human abilities
   • learning to trust God instead of getting upset when
     things happen that you don't like

   _____

   _____

   _____

5. What seemingly impossible situation do you need God
   to change in your life? How do the stories and scriptures in this chapter help build your faith that He is
   able to do the impossible?

   _____

   _____

   _____

CHAPTER 4

The Key to Transformation

The Bible is God's chart for you to steer by, to keep you from the bottom of the sea, and to show you where the harbor is, and how to reach it without running on rocks or bars.

Henry Ward Beecher[2]

The word *transformed* means "to change completely the appearance or character of something or someone, especially so that that thing or person is improved."[3] I can say without hesitation that I have been transformed. I am a radically different person today than I was forty-seven years ago. When I think or speak about my childhood and all the abuse I endured, I feel I am talking not about myself but about someone I knew long ago. That old person died with Christ and has been resurrected to a new life.

I often say Dave has been married to about twenty different women, because he married me when I was a huge mess and has been with me through my journey of change, which has come in stages. About the time Dave gets used to me one way, God changes me again, and he must get introduced to a different—but better—version of me.

God will change you also if you will let Him. Each of us has free will, and God will not force us to do anything. He tells us in His Word what is good for us and what His plan is, and He wants us to use our free will to choose His will.

Many of the changes in me have involved the breaking of self-will and rebellion toward male authority because of the ways men abused me. Control was probably the most difficult thing for me to let go of because I was afraid that, if I wasn't in control, I would get hurt. You may also struggle with wanting to be in control. But now I realize that trying to control everyone and everything in my life is hard work, and I am glad that God helped me to see that it isn't my job. He is in control, and if we fight that fact, we will always be frustrated and struggling. Fighting God is a losing battle.

Transformation or complete change happens little by little, and it's something we must be committed to for life. I am still changing, and I still need to change more. It is not all easy, but I have learned that the sooner we submit to God's will, the less it will hurt. Self-will in us must die so the life of Christ can live in us. Paul writes, "It is no longer I who live, but Christ lives in me" (Galatians 2:20 NKJV). We don't have to struggle trying to get what we want because God will give us what is right for us if we delight ourselves in Him (Psalm 37:4).

> *Transformation happens little by little, so you must commit to it for life.*

I was a broken, dysfunctional person when I finally began to let God work in me, and just as a caterpillar is transformed into a beautiful one-of-a-kind butterfly, God has transformed me. God has worked to change me in many ways and taught me many lessons through each of the changes.

I hope that what I share in this book about the transformation God has done in me is a great encouragement to you. What God will do for one person He will do for another, if we will only believe and live according to His Word.

Transformation Comes by Renewing Your Mind

In the previous chapter, I emphasized the importance of changing your thinking to agree with God's thinking as represented in His Word. In our relationship with God, learning to renew—or change—our minds is vital if we want to deal with the changes that can take place in our lives in a positive way. In fact, it is the key to transformation. Romans 12:2 says:

> Do not be conformed to this world (this age), [fashioned after and adapted to its external, superficial customs], but be transformed (changed) by the [entire] renewal of your mind [by its new ideals and its new attitude], so that you may prove [for yourselves] what is the good and acceptable and perfect will of God, even the thing which is good and acceptable and perfect [in His sight for you].

I believe this scripture teaches that if we want to experience God's good will for our lives, we must learn to think the way He thinks. His Word represents His thoughts. So, we must learn the Word and let the Holy Spirit work with us to transform (change or renew) our minds.

For years, I listened to sermons and heard about the good life God wants us to have as Christians. He wants us to live with peace, joy, and growth in all areas—spiritually, mentally, physically, emotionally, financially, socially, and other ways. I agreed with this because it is based on John 10:10 and 3 John 2, but I was not experiencing it in my daily life. I didn't feel I was growing spiritually, or if I was, the growth was extremely slow. I worried, I was fearful, and I dreaded doing many of the things I needed to do. I was tired and often didn't feel well. I was emotionally unstable, and my moods fluctuated because I allowed my circumstances to dictate them. I did have some good times, but they seemed to be frequently interrupted by trials and difficulties. Our family struggled financially, and although we were able to pay our bills, we lived from paycheck to paycheck and regularly needed a miracle from God to cover unexpected expenses, even though we tithed faithfully (gave 10 percent of our income to God's work). Socially, many friends rejected us when I began teaching God's Word because they felt I was prideful and out of God's will. This was in 1976, when only a handful of women were teaching the Bible, and people didn't accept it easily. In the midst of this, I kept hearing that God wants good things for His people.

Although I saw in God's Word that Jesus died so we could have life and have it more abundantly (John 10:10), my thinking was based on my circumstances, not on God's Word. I had a lot of trouble and expected more trouble. I felt my entire life had been one of misery, fear, and dealing with one problem after another. This was the way I thought, and until I learned how important it is to allow my mind to be renewed according to God's Word, I had no idea that my thinking—or my life—could change.

Our ways of thinking are ingrained in us. We have been practicing them for many years, and even though we may want to change our minds, actu-

Change in your life begins with change in your thoughts.

ally doing so takes time and practice. It also requires dedication to studying, confessing, and meditating on God's Word. It's important to remember that change in our lives begins with change in our thoughts.

You may think as I once did that you can't do anything about what you think. Thoughts come into your mind, and you accept them as your own, but many of them are put there by the devil. Anything that doesn't agree with God's Word is to be cast down by us and replaced with something that is in God's Word. As you learn to recognize the lies of Satan, you will experience more and more victory.

The Holy Spirit Helps Us

As we learn God's Word, the Holy Spirit will remind us of it when we are thinking ungodly thoughts. For example, if someone has hurt me, and I think about what they did to me and how upset I am and make plans to shut them out of my life so they cannot hurt me again, the Holy Spirit will interrupt this train of thought and remind me that God wants me to forgive and pray for my enemies (Matthew 5:44; Mark 11:25). At this point, I have a decision to make: Will I obey God or let my feelings lead me to keep going my own way? My unrenewed mind tells me that forgiving them wouldn't be fair, but God's Word says I must trust Him to be my Vindicator (Romans 12:19). He will be sure I am rewarded for the decision to obey Him instead of doing what I want to do (Luke 11:28).

Being obedient to God and following His will instead of our personal desires is the key to living a successful Christian life. Anytime an area of our lives needs adjusting, we have to do something differently from how we are currently doing it. It requires change. We want our circumstances to change, but quite often the change needs to start in us.

Perhaps I am planning a major purchase, such as a house or a new car, but I haven't prayed about it or even acknowledged God in my plan. I am skeptical when the Holy Spirit reminds me that I need to pray about the purchase before making it. I may not want to pray because I am afraid I won't get what I want, so I have a decision to make: Will I pray and choose God's will even if it isn't what I want, or will I press on toward my own desires and simply do as I please?

If we decide to surrender our will to God, our lives can be wonderfully glorious. But I admit that thinking about spending our entire lives never knowing if we will get what we want can be a bit frightening. At least that's the way the natural person thinks. Experience with God teaches us that His will is always best. We may not think so initially, but time teaches us that it is. Many times, God does give us what we want, but if He doesn't give us what we want, it is because He has something better in mind and is waiting for us to come into agreement with Him.

Thoughts Are Powerful

For the weapons of our warfare are not physical [weapons of flesh and blood], but they are mighty before God for the overthrow and destruction of strongholds, [inasmuch as we] refute arguments and theories and reasonings and every proud and lofty thing that sets itself up against the [true] knowledge of God; and we lead every thought and purpose away captive into the obedience of Christ (the Messiah, the Anointed One).

2 Corinthians 10:4–5

Thoughts that are according to the true knowledge of God (His Word) are weapons of warfare, and they pull down the mental strongholds (areas dominated by an enemy, in the believer's case, Satan) built in our minds before we knew the truth of God's Word.

Second Corinthians 10:4–5 proves that we can do our own thinking. We don't have to think whatever falls into our mind; we can cast down (reject) ungodly thoughts and replace them with godly ones.

We have been given the mind of Christ and "hold the thoughts (feelings and purposes) of His heart" (1 Corinthians 2:16). Since the mind of Christ is in us, we can think according to it if we choose to. Paul writes that "the mind of the flesh [which is sense and reason without the Holy Spirit] is death [death that comprises all the miseries arising from sin, both here and hereafter]. But the mind of the [Holy] Spirit is life and [soul] peace [both now and forever]" (Romans 8:6).

> Pay attention to the condition of your mind.

As you deal with the changes in your life, pay attention to the condition of your mind. Is it confused or peaceful, worried, passive, busy, decisive, fragmented, double-minded, critical, suspicious, positive, negative, or filled with condemnation? Do your thoughts minister life or death to you? Is your mind focused or wandering? Our minds may be in many various conditions, and we should make sure they are filled with good thoughts that will minister life and power to us.

Staying mentally sharp and focused is important. Are you able to keep your mind on what you are doing? A lot of people aren't.

> One article states that "The average human attention span is 8.25 seconds. Attention spans can range from 2 seconds to over 20 minutes. The average human attention

span decreased by almost 25% from 2000 to 2015. Humans have shorter attention spans than goldfish (9 seconds)."[4]

I think we can increase our attention span as we practice keeping our minds on what we are doing and refusing to let them wander. We will need God's help to do this, but it can be done.

Get Ready to Be Transformed

The more you renew your mind according to God's Word, the better equipped you will be when you face life's changes. God doesn't do anything at random, and when He brings or allows changes in our lives, it's for a purpose, and it's intended for good. As we grow in knowing His Word and thinking according to His thoughts, we also grow in our ability to navigate change in positive, productive ways.

Questions

1. Based on the meaning of the word *transformed*, how has God transformed you?

_____

_____

_____

2. Explain why the mind is the key to transformation and why "change in our lives begins with change in our thoughts."

_____

_____

_____

3. How would you assess the condition of your mind right now, and what needs to change about the way you think?

_____

_____

_____

4. How does God's Word help us deal with the changes we face in life?

_____

_____

_____

CHAPTER 5

Adjust Your Attitude

If you don't like something, change it. If you can't change it, change your attitude.

Maya Angelou[5]

Our attitude is the lens through which we see the world. It is our thoughts turned inside out, and the apostle Paul writes that we are "to be made new in the attitude of" our minds (Ephesians 4:23 NIV). Thoughts may be private, but the people around us can see our attitude. If I have a negative attitude, it means I am thinking about what I don't like about my life, what I don't have, or other negative situations. If I have a positive attitude, it means I am thinking about all the good things in my life, how thankful I am for them, and how happy I am. I believe each of us has more good things in our lives than bad things. We simply need to see them and think about the good things instead of the bad things.

> *Think about the good things in your life instead of the bad things.*

Attitudes That Can Help Us Deal with Change

Our attitude makes a big difference in the way we deal with change. A positive attitude toward change will help us handle it well, while a negative attitude is likely to cause us to struggle. While we should endeavor to maintain a generally positive attitude toward change, a portion of Jesus' Sermon on the Mount called the Beatitudes (Matthew 5:1–12) points out several specific attitudes we should have.

In the Beatitudes, Jesus teaches us eight ways to be blessed. I like to refer to these as "The Be-Attitudes" because they help us see how we need to *be* and the *attitudes* we need if we want to live a blessed life. Some people don't think change is a blessing at all, but this is not true. It is a healthy, positive aspect of growing and becoming everything God wants us to be and being able to do all He wants us to do. You *can* be blessed in the midst of change. This is God's desire, and a good attitude will help you do it.

We read in the Beatitudes that there are several qualities people need in order to please God and have an enjoyable life. In fact, it says that the people who develop these qualities will be blessed. In Matthew 5:3 in the Amplified Bible, Classic Edition, the word *blessed* is amplified this way: "happy, to be envied, and spiritually prosperous—with life-joy and satisfaction in God's favor and salvation, regardless of their outward conditions." I am quite sure we all want this description to apply to us, and God's Word tells us how to get it.

Meekness (Matthew 5:5)

One typical response many people have when they face change is to resist it, especially if they did not initiate it.

> Be open to change, realizing that it may turn out well.

They immediately think, *I don't want to do this someone else's way. I want to keep doing it my way!* This kind of thinking represents a prideful attitude, which only makes people stubborn and resistant to change. When we have an attitude of meekness, we are open to change and willing to try something new or different, realizing that it may turn out well.

In Scripture, we read more about being humble than about being meek, but the attitudes of meekness and humility are similar. When I think of them, I am reminded of 1 Peter 5:6: "Therefore humble yourselves [demote, lower yourselves in your own estimation] under the mighty hand of God, that in due time He may exalt you." When we are meek and humble, we trust God. We don't take matters into our own hands, even when we don't understand the changes that are taking place. First Peter 5:7 says, "Casting the whole of your care [all your anxieties, all your worries, all your concerns, once and for all] on Him, for He cares for you affectionately and cares about you watchfully." When we worry, it means we think we can solve our own problems if we think about them long enough. That's not being meek and humble.

Jesus was meek and humble. He didn't have to go to the cross and suffer as He did, but He chose to do so because He knew it was God's will. In Matthew 11:29 He says we should take His yoke and learn from Him because He is "gentle (meek) and humble (lowly) in heart." I think it's safe to say that we see few people with such attitudes in our world today.

Yesterday, when our daughter parked her car at the grocery store, she accidently cut in front of another car she didn't see. The man she cut off followed her, parked his car, got out, and yelled at her. She apologized, said she was very sorry, and explained that she had not seen him. He continued yelling and told her she was a liar. He was *not* being meek or humble! He must be a very angry person. He vented his anger on her, but I doubt she was the sole source of it. The world is filled with angry people, and I think a lot of this is because instinctively people know something is wrong in our world today and they haven't yet found the answer in Jesus.

> Put on meekness and humility as you would your clothing.

According to 1 Peter 5:5, we are to clothe ourselves with humility. In other words, we are to wear humility like a garment. Just as we deliberately put on our clothing, we must also deliberately put on meekness and humility. These attitudes go against natural human nature, but they are possible for the person who has received Jesus and has the help of the Holy Spirit.

Proverbs 16:18 says, "Pride goes before destruction, and a haughty spirit before a fall." This scripture tells us plainly that when we experience destruction or failure, it is often caused by pride and a haughty spirit—the opposite of meekness. God gives grace to those who are humble, but He resists the proud (James 4:6).

The account of King Nebuchadnezzar of Babylon is a perfect example of how humility brings blessings, but pride brings destruction. In Daniel 4:1–37, we read that King Nebuchadnezzar gave God all the praise and glory for his successes. He was at home in his palace—contented, prosperous, and at rest. But a year later, he began taking credit for himself for all the good things God was doing during his reign (Daniel 4:30). As a result, he lost his kingdom and wandered as a wild animal in the wilderness until he came to his right mind, turned back to God, and began glorifying Him again (Daniel 4:37). God restored his honor and splendor, and his kingdom was even greater than before. Once again, we see the great mercy of God. Nebuchadnezzar sinned, but as soon as he repented, God forgave him and blessed him more than even before. This should be encouraging to anyone who has sinned and may mistakenly believe that they cannot be forgiven or that their life will never be as good as it once was.

Each day offers opportunities for us to have a meek, humble attitude. When change comes to your life, you can choose to resist it or you can choose to face it with humility and meekness, trusting that God knows exactly what is best for you and is leading you through every change as He fulfills His good plan for your life. Andrew Murray wrote that humility "must be made the object of special prayer."[6] It is one of the most difficult attitudes to attain and maintain. But all things are possible with God (Matthew 19:26).

Mercy (Matthew 5:7)

Having a merciful attitude, which involves being loving, gracious, and forgiving toward others, is being like Christ, and it brings a blessing. Proverbs 11:17 says, "A merciful person does himself good, but the cruel person does himself harm" (NASB). If we have a merciful attitude toward others, we will be shown mercy (Matthew 5:7). Anyone can be judgmental, but mercy is greater than judgment (James 2:13).

God is rich in mercy because of the great love with which He loves us (Ephesians 2:4–5). As believers in Jesus, we are instructed over and over in God's Word to love others (Mark 12:31; John 13:34; Romans 13:8). If we love them, we will show them mercy. When we walk in obedience to God's Word and His will, our hearts are filled with joy and peace. But when we don't, they feel heavy and burdened, guilty and condemned.

One way to show mercy is to forgive when we believe whoever hurt us is in the wrong and doesn't deserve to be forgiven. We all make mistakes frequently—little ones and sometimes big ones—and we need mercy. If we are not willing to show people mercy, we will live miserable and lonely lives. We may justify ourselves when we refuse to show mercy, but true justification only comes from God.

> Show mercy, or you will live a miserable and lonely life.

When people offend or hurt us, we may soothe ourselves by meditating on the other person's offense, but it is the glory of man to overlook offenses (Proverbs 19:11). We may think that if we show mercy, we are inviting the person who hurt us to do it again, but we should always trust God in such situations. If people continue to hurt us over and over, God will deal with them. God will always take care of us if we are willing to do things His way. Anyone can be harsh and hard-hearted, but only someone who is full of God's Spirit can show mercy and kindness to someone who doesn't deserve it. Showing someone forgiveness and mercy doesn't always mean restoring a relationship, especially if the offending party is abusive. It does mean that our attitude toward them changes and that we pray for them. People who are hurting hurt people, and if we remember this, it is easier to be merciful.

God's mercy amazes me. We can do the most awful things, but because of His mercy, sincere repentance restores us to God as though we have never done anything wrong. God wants us to demonstrate to others the same attitude of mercy He has toward us.

> Sincere repentance restores us to God.

Purity of Heart (Matthew 5:8)

A pure heart has no selfish motives. People who are pure in heart don't do anything to call attention to themselves or to put others in their debt. Whether they work hard, show kindness, give gifts, do good deeds, or pray, they do these things with humility and sincerity, not to be seen or well thought of. They do them because they love God and want to do what Jesus would do in similar situations.

People with pure hearts do everything they do with pure motives. They give to give, not to get. They do all they do as though they are doing it for the Lord, and not for the sake of people-pleasing. Those with pure-hearted attitudes seek God for who He is, not for what He can do for them. They seek His face (meaning His presence), not His hand (meaning what He can do for them).

Keeping a pure heart requires constant diligence because the heart is deceitful above all else (Jeremiah 17:9). When we are born again, God does give us a new heart, and He puts His Spirit in us, but we must choose to operate out of that heart and not allow the old nature (the one we lived in before receiving Christ) to control us. Living with a pure heart requires continually making godly choices. The Holy Spirit will help us by making us aware of any wrong motives we have if we want Him to, but it is up to us to follow His guidance. He will not violate our free will and force us to do what is right.

> Living with a pure heart requires making godly choices.

David prayed for a clean heart: "Create in me a clean heart, O God, and renew a right spirit within me" (Psalm 51:10 ESV). And Paul writes that our goal should be love that comes from a pure heart and a good conscience (1 Timothy 1:5). As you embrace the process of change, I pray you will do it with a pure heart and that you will reap the benefits and blessings of this godly attitude.

Change is rarely easy, but a positive attitude, such as the ones mentioned in this chapter, will help you navigate it successfully.

Questions

1. How does a person with a negative attitude think? How does someone with a positive attitude think?

   _____

   _____

   _____

2. How can you incorporate the three Be-Attitudes mentioned in this chapter into your life?

   _____

   _____

   _____

3. When has someone shown you mercy? How did you feel?

   _____

   _____

   _____

4. Who needs you to show mercy to them right now, and how will you do it?

   _____

   _____

   _____

CHAPTER 6

Stay at Peace

*Do not lose your inner peace for anything whatso-
ever, even if your whole world seems upset.*

St. Francis de Sales[7]

Jesus says in Matthew 5:9, "Blessed are the peacemakers, for they will be called children of God" (NIV). When we live with a calm, peaceful attitude that seeks peace within ourselves and peace in the atmosphere around us, we are truly blessed. Times of change may be unsettling in many ways, and we will navigate them much better if we stay at peace internally and become peacemakers in the situations around us.

I lived many years of my life without peace because I let myself get upset when things did not go my way. People and circumstances that annoyed me made me angry, and angry people do not enjoy peace. I wanted my circumstances to be peaceful, but I finally realized that I was the one who had to be peaceful even amid unenjoyable circumstances.

Jesus says that He gives us His peace—not a peace like the world gives, but *His* peace (John 14:27). This peace is present amid the worst of circumstances. The amplification of this scripture says that because He gives us His peace, we are to stop allowing ourselves to be "agitated and disturbed," and we should not permit ourselves to be "fearful and intimidated and cowardly and unsettled." In other words, we are not to let ourselves stay upset, even though we may be tempted to do so when things are changing in our lives.

God has given us what we need to live in peace, but we must access it and calm our souls when they are stirred with anger, worry, or fear. We can do this by thinking about God's deliverance instead of our current problems. We can also do it by remembering past victories. When you become upset, have a talk with yourself and remind yourself that being upset won't do any good but is likely to do a lot of harm. When we are upset, we place stress on ourselves. This makes us tired and often sick. In addition, it can cause us to say things that we later wish we could take back.

When we are going through changes, we may feel more emotional than usual, and out-of-control emotions are dangerous. But with God's help, we can regain our peace and be stable rather than erratic.

When a problem disrupts the peace between you and another person, be quick to apologize. I think the person who apologizes first is often the one who is strongest spiritually. If there is strife between you and anyone else at this time in your life, why not settle it now? Be the peace-maker by making the first move to restore peace in your relationships. This requires humility because the conflict may not be your fault, but being a peacemaker is a sign of spiritual maturity. Romans 12:18 tells us, "If possible, so far as it depends on you, live peaceably with all" (ESV). We cannot force people to be at peace with us, but we can choose to be at peace with them.

> You deserve peace, so access the peace Jesus has given.

You deserve peace, so why not access the peace Jesus has given you?

Isaiah 26:3 says about God: "You keep him in perfect peace whose mind is stayed on you, because he trusts in you" (ESV). Based on this verse, I believe the thoughts we allow in our minds determine our level of peace. This is why I say to have a talk with yourself when you are upset. You can talk yourself into being upset by thinking upsetting thoughts, and you can talk yourself into peace by thinking peaceful thoughts.

First Peter 3:11 says we must turn from evil, seek peace, and pursue it. This scripture has had a powerful effect in my life. It helped me realize that peace is not an automatic experience; it must be pursued. We can't even simply pray for it; we must do the things that will cause it. If I am not at peace, there may be various reasons for my upset. Perhaps there is sin hidden in my heart, and I need to talk with God about it. Or maybe I am doing something outside of God's will. I may be angry with someone and need to forgive them, or I may be frustrated because something didn't go the way I wanted it to, and I need to trust God in that circumstance. Maybe I have heard bad news or am upset about something that has happened to someone. We can always find our way back to a state of peace if we will follow the Holy Spirit's guidance. Instead of worrying and being anxious about our problems, we should pray about them and give thanks for all the wonderful blessings in our lives. Then peace will fill our hearts (Philippians 4:6–7).

Don't Let Anything Steal Your Peace

No doubt, peace is extremely valuable to us, especially when everything around us is changing and we feel uncertain or wonder if it will all turn out all right. I would say peace is precious, and we need to guard it diligently. Life is miserable without peace. Various thoughts, emotions, and attitudes can steal our peace if we let them. These include anger and worry, which I wrote about in the previous chapter. They also include fear, and emotions such as jealousy and bitterness. I think most of us recognize all of these as threats to our peace.

Before I close this chapter, I want to mention two attitudes that aren't often viewed as ones that steal our peace, but they do: selfishness and self-pity. When dealing with change, we will surely struggle if we think about ourselves and our desires excessively or if we feel sorry for ourselves or develop a victim mentality. It is impossible to have a good life with a bad attitude. The goal of change is to help us have a good life, and we can't have one if we are selfish or if we constantly feel sorry for ourselves.

> *You cannot have a good life with a bad attitude.*

I won't elaborate on selfishness here because I believe most people understand it and are aware of its dangers. I have written an entire book on overcoming selfishness, called *What About Me?*, which explains why selfishness is so bad for us and what we can do to break free from it. For now, let's just remember what Paul writes in Philippians 2:3–5 (AMP):

> Do nothing from selfishness or empty conceit [through factional motives, or strife], but with [an attitude of] humility [being neither arrogant nor self-righteous], regard others as more important than yourselves. Do not merely look out for your own personal interests, but also for the interests of others. Have this same attitude in yourselves which was in Christ Jesus [look to Him as your example in selfless humility].

For the remainder of this chapter, I'd like to focus on how self-pity steals our peace and makes change unnecessarily difficult to manage.

Self-pity is a destructive attitude, and it makes us miserable. It is idolatry (meaning the worship of someone or something other than God) because when we wallow in self-pity, we focus only on ourselves. For years, I had such a huge problem with self-pity that I feel I could have earned a master's degree in it. But God dealt with me about it, and over time, He has graciously set me free from it.

Self-pity is a destructive attitude.

I felt sorry for myself for many reasons—because I was abused as a child, because my first husband cheated on me, because I didn't think Dave paid enough attention to me, because I thought I did all the work around the house while everyone else had fun, and for other reasons. For years, I wasted days on end feeling sorry for myself. Anytime I didn't get my way, I became angry and then felt sorry for myself. I usually withdrew from my family, isolated myself, and thought about how badly I was being treated. The list of situations that caused me to feel sorry for myself was endless. I needed to change, but I had to change my mind to change my attitude. Most of my self-pity was rooted in my general negative attitude. I leaned toward being negative instead of positive, and I am so grateful that God changed me. Being negative is self-torment, but it can change.

My attitude put my self-pitying thoughts on display, but the problem began in my thinking. My mind was a dark place filled with negative things I imagined were happening to me. This depressed me and left me feeling sorry for myself when I could have chosen to be thankful for what I had and let my gratitude lead me to enjoy my life. Because I was stuck in self-pity, I could not receive the healing God wanted to bring to me.

I know from experience that self-pity is a choice we make. It may be based on circumstances—circumstances we have blown out of proportion and meditated on until they have consumed us and left us feeling sorry for ourselves. Self-pity has never and will never do anyone any good. It never helps a situation, but it does make us feel that circumstances are worse than they actually are. When we need to deal with change, self-pity keeps us focused on the difficult or challenging aspects of it, when we need to be focused on the positive things the change will bring to our lives.

Self-pity also has a negative impact on our ability to trust God. It has nothing to do with faith, and if we want God to help us, we need to ask for His help in faith. God may have compassion for us, but He won't pity us because He knows He can change anything. We simply need to trust Him to do so. Psalm 103:13 says, "As a father pities his children, so the Lord pities those who fear Him" (NKJV). But this verse is talking about something different than merely feeling sorry for us. God's compassion moves Him to help us. When we feel sorry for ourselves or try to get God to feel sorry for us, we don't really want help, or we are frustrated with the help we are getting because it isn't what we want. We simply want to feel pitiful.

Replace self-pity with gratitude.

I encourage you to replace self-pity with an attitude of gratitude. One of the best attitudes we can have is one of thankfulness, while one of the worst is self-pity. God does so much for us that we should never stop thanking Him. We all have many reasons to be thankful, and we should remember them. We must have a thankful heart to enter the presence of God (Psalm 100:4). We are to present our petitions to God with a thankful heart (Philippians 4:6). Being thankful is powerful. It makes us happy, people enjoy being around us, it puts a smile on God's face, it is a key to answered prayer, and it is God's will (1 Thessalonians 5:18).

No matter how many problems you may have, they don't outweigh your blessings. Remember this when you are tempted to feel sorry for yourself. If you don't see your blessings, it is because you are not looking for them. The dark glasses of pity are clouding your view. I believe self-pity is a sin that needs to be repented of, so if you have been feeling sorry for yourself, spend some time with God and ask for His forgiveness. Replace self-pity with the power of thanksgiving.

I am eternally grateful that God has delivered me from the foolishness of self-pity. It never makes a situation better; it only makes us feel worse. As you face changes in your life, whether you initiate them or not, I hope you can see from this chapter how important it is to stay at peace and resist self-pity.

Questions

1. The opening quotation of this chapter, by St. Francis de Sales, says "Do not lose your inner peace for anything whatsoever, even if your whole world seems upset." Why is this powerful advice?

_____

_____

_____

2. How is the peace Jesus gives different from the peace
   the world gives?

   _____

   _____

   _____

3. First Peter 3:11 says we must turn from evil, seek peace,
   and pursue it. How can you intentionally pursue peace
   in your life?

   _____

   _____

   _____

4. What are your biggest peace-stealers? Perhaps rela-
   tional conflict, job stress, finances, watching too much
   television or not making good choices about what you
   watch or listen to, overcommitment, poor time man-
   agement, or something else? How can you stop letting
   these things or situations rob you of your peace?

   _____

   _____

   _____

5. How do selfishness and self-pity steal our peace?

   _____

   _____

   _____

PART 3

Managing Change Well

CHAPTER 7

Little by Little

It's difficult to change overnight but if you are persistent and take one step at a time you will see results!

Jack LaLanne[8]

Most changes that take place in the growth process don't happen quickly. They unfold over time. I believe this is so we can learn to handle each new opportunity and responsibility God gives us. As we continue to learn and grow, He continues to gives us more.

Years ago, I had a great desire to teach God's Word all over the world. But God didn't see my desire and immediately launch me into a global teaching ministry. He has led me one step at a time so He could prepare me for greater influence and responsibility. Sometimes His leading seemed painfully slow, and I now realize that He worked so carefully and deliberately with me because He wanted me to succeed in ministry and enjoy it, but He also knew I needed to be strengthened and seasoned along the way. If success comes too quickly, it often makes us prideful—and pride comes before destruction (Proverbs 16:18).

The same is true for you. Whether your God-given dream pertains to ministry or to something else, God wants you to have the stability, wisdom, and stamina to manage it successfully and be fulfilled in it—and this requires a gradual process that plays out over a period of time.

God loves us too much to throw us into situations we cannot handle. That's why He leads us through changes step-by-step. I often say that some people have a gift that can take them somewhere, but they don't have enough character to keep them there. I believe the ministry God has given me has grown to where it is today in six stages. Hopefully, learning how He has taken one woman's desire and grown it into a large organization that reaches

> Some people have a gift that can take them somewhere but not enough character to keep them there.

around the world will encourage you to believe He can do anything for you and to recognize how and when He is changing things to take you to the next level of your destiny.

Stage 1

The first stage of ministry for me involved teaching one home Bible study for two-and-a-half years and being faithful to that, then adding a second Bible study for another two-and-a-half years, for a total of five years. I was not paid during this time, even though our family's financial situation was dire. People who attended the Bible studies occasionally gave me a little money, but usually very little, and no one gave regularly. God did meet our family's needs, but this period of time stretched our faith—and that was vital for our future.

Stage 2

The second stage for me was to stop teaching both Bible studies and do nothing. When God led me to stop teaching,

I felt something big would happen for me quickly, but it didn't. Instead, I spent an entire year waiting for God to open the next door. I thought nothing was happening during that year, but as I look back, I now realize that God did a lot in me. Often, God must do something *in* us before He can do something *through* us. That year, one of the big lessons I learned was that I had to be myself. I couldn't be someone else. I couldn't do what anyone else did the way they did it. I tried to do many things I saw other people doing during that season, but none of them worked for me. I could do nothing but wait and hope I had not been foolish to give up the Bible studies.

> God must do something in you before He can do something through you.

The devil was telling me I needed to be a "regular woman" (whatever that is), and I tried sewing, gardening, and other things I thought regular women did. But I hated them and was terrible at them. I had to get the idea of being a regular woman out of my mind before God could use me as He wanted. I finally came to the conclusion that being a regular woman was doing whatever God wanted for me, even though it was different from what most other women I knew were doing.

Stage 3

The third phase of the ministry took place when our family started attending a new church near our home. It was small, only thirty people, when we began going there. But after a while, the church grew, and the pastor invited me to teach a women's Bible study in the church. I said yes and prepared for it as though a thousand would show up. A thousand people didn't come, but 110 did, and that was a miracle, since there were not 110 people in the entire church. Word about the Bible study had spread, and obviously, God prompted people to come, because they didn't know me at all.

That Bible study was held every Thursday, and it eventually led to my being offered a full-time job on staff at the church, where I fulfilled a variety of responsibilities. The weekly meeting grew to more than four hundred ladies, and during the five years I led it, I learned many lessons. I became an associate pastor at the church and was allowed to teach when the pastor was out of town. I also taught in the church's Bible school three times a week, counseled people, and learned a lot about leadership. After five years in the associate pastor position, I felt a stirring in my heart to move on, but it frightened me because I thought, *If I give this up and I'm wrong, then I will have nothing.*

I wanted to do more than I was doing in my role at the church. I wanted to write books and travel to speak at other places, and to do so, I had to leave that position. Due to fear, I waited almost two years to resign. During that time, I became more and more miserable. I lost interest in what was going on at the church, and it was a very confusing time for me. I had received many confirmations that I needed to leave and start a ministry, but I didn't want to be prideful or to act on mere ambition. I truly wanted what I did to be God's will.

My pastor noticed that something wasn't right and suggested that I take some time off and pray about what God wanted me to do. I did, and God spoke clearly within half a day that I was to take the ministry and go north, south, east, and west. With the word from God came a strong desire to reach more people, so I finally did quit my job. Although I wanted change, I was also frightened.

We lived in St. Louis, Missouri, and I didn't know what to do to take the ministry "north, south, east, and west," so Dave and I started meetings in north St. Louis, south St. Louis, east St. Louis, and west St. Louis. We went on eight radio stations with a fifteen-minute teaching program and prayed for invitations for speaking engagements. None came for quite some time, so we were faithful to do the weekly and monthly meetings we had organized.

The attendance at our meetings was meager. We used the offerings from the meetings to support the ministry, although at the time the expenses were not much. Our first employee volunteered for a couple of years before we actually hired her, and her first salary was fifty dollars per week. My second employee used a large cardboard box for her desk. I recall once having a hundred people at one of our meetings, and we were so excited we felt we had died and gone to heaven.

Stage 4

The fourth stage of the ministry involved getting my teachings broadcast on as many radio stations as possible. Eventually, we were on one hundred stations. As our radio audience grew, we went to the cities where the stations were located and held meetings in hotel ballrooms. The typical attendance in those meetings was between two hundred and three hundred people. We worked so hard in those days that when I look back on them, I wonder how we survived. But God's grace was on us because He always gives us the strength to do what He calls us to do.

As the years went by, we hired a few more people and eventually moved the ministry out of the basement of our home to a 1,700-square-foot space we rented in an office complex. It seemed huge to us at the time, and we wondered what we would do with so much room. But before long, it was filled and we needed more space.

Stage 5

The fifth stage of the ministry began when we started our television broadcast. At first, my teachings aired once a week, then eventually they were broadcast daily. Once this happened, the ministry grew by about one-third each year. Each time someone moved out of the office complex, we rented their space until eventually we occupied almost all the space in the building and started looking for a building to purchase.

Nothing we tried worked out, and eventually we bought some property and started preparations to build a building. Dave had been in the engineering field, so he drew the plans, and we started a building program, asking people to donate to help fund the construction. We determined we would not borrow money, so it took a lot of time to complete the project, but we finally did. We now have almost 200,000 square feet of space for our headquarters as well as offices in several countries outside the United States.

We were eventually on television in about two-thirds of the world in more than 110 languages, and Dave and I were getting older and more tired all the time. We had the big ministry we wanted, and at one time we had nine hundred employees. But keeping up with everything was wearing me out. Each year, I probably spoke more than two hundred times and wrote two or three books, plus being involved in managing the offices. I also traveled internationally twice a year for two to three weeks at a time and held crusades and various outreaches in different countries. I recall one time going to Australia and teaching twenty-one times in twenty days. Needless to say, I was exhausted by the time I returned home.

Stage 6

The sixth stage of our ministry began when I started delegating tasks and responsibilities to other people and personally taking on only what I can do—writing my books (which total over 150 as of the writing of this book), recording our television program, and teaching at our conferences. In some ways, this has been the most difficult transition for me because I have had to let go of things I birthed and watch other people do them. Sometimes people don't do them the way I would, but many times they have better and fresher ideas than I would have.

Our two sons now manage the daily activities of the ministry. One is the CEO of Hand of Hope and handles all the mission outreaches, which include foreign television, outreaches to help provide medical and dental care, an inner-city church, a residential recovery center for men seeking freedom from alcohol and drug addiction, the digging of water wells in villages that have no clean water, building churches, and so much more. Our other son is the CEO of all the media and ministry operations, as well as a large ranch in Utah that will be a base for victims of sex trafficking. Our two sons have different giftings and personalities, and each one is well suited for the responsibilities he has. Both sons have very big jobs, and they both do a very good job. Had I been unwilling to accept change and delegate responsibilities within the ministry to others, I never would have seen my two sons blossom and grow in the ways I have.

> *Change is not just doing new things but letting go of old things.*

Change not only involves taking on new things, but it also often involves letting go of old things.

Give It Time

Getting accustomed to change takes time. When we hire people in our ministry, they often move from other states to come to work for us. This has been hard on some of them. Most have stayed and started a new life, but some have quit and returned home. Some people navigate change better than others do, and each of us must do what we can handle.

When people move, they lose their personal interaction with their friends, their church, their old job, and their old home. Everything is new, and they must get used to it. In some ways, this is exciting, but in other ways, it is difficult.

A person's personality type helps determine how difficult change will or won't be. Some people are more adventurous than others. I am bold and aggressive, but I am not going to do some things that some of my friends do, such as hang gliding, parachuting out of an airplane, cliff diving, swimming with sharks, or other things that I have no desire to do. I'll face a crowd of one million people and boldly proclaim the gospel, but if I see a mouse, I scream. ☺

One man I know said he would never understand how a woman could pour hot wax on her lip and rip out the hairs with tape but scream when she sees a spider. I guess it depends on desire. I don't desire to jump out of an airplane, but I do desire to teach the Word of God, and I desire not to have a hairy lip.

Time does soothe a lot of our fears. We do adjust to change and usually end up liking it. I am now accomplishing more for the kingdom of God than ever before, and I am working less. I am working smarter instead of harder, and that's because I let go of certain tasks and responsibilities that I really don't have to fulfill any longer. Don't ever be afraid to give up the good to get the great. Some people absolutely hate change, and this is a shame because we cannot grow without change. No change means no growth. Robin Sharma said, "Don't live the same year 75 times and call it a life."[9]

> "Don't live the same year 75 times and call it a life."
> —Robin Sharma

John F. Kennedy said, "Change is the law of life. And those who look only to the past or present are certain to miss the future."[10] Any change, even a change for the better, is accompanied by discomfort. Change is painful, but nothing is as painful as never changing. Staying stuck in the same place doing the same thing forever gets boring for anybody. You can't change unless you step out of your comfort zone and realize that, in time, the change will feel comfortable.

The time it takes to change can be likened to a slow-cooked roast compared to a quick trip through a fast-food restaurant. One is easier, but the other is better. Don't always choose the easy road. Jesus didn't, and neither should we.

Some people grieve deeply when their children leave home, but it will happen to every parent. Wise parents plan for this transition and aren't devastated when the time comes. They often grieve because things are not the same for them, and they now need to find something to put themselves into besides their children. They will have to try something new.

When we think of trying something we have never done, we usually ask ourselves, *What if I don't like it or am not good at it?* This doesn't have to be a problem, because if it happens, you can always try something else. You may be surprised to find that there are far better things ahead than you leave behind and that each change you face holds its own blessings.

Questions

1. What dream or purpose has God given you that may require you to change?

_____

_____

_____

2. If you feel stuck in an in-between stage, what is God saying for you to do as you wait? Why is it always

important to be yourself, no matter where you are in
your journey?

_____

_____

_____

3. What old things do you need to let go of in order to
   embrace new things?

_____

_____

_____

4. How does knowing that each change holds its own
   blessings help you be willing to try something new?

_____

_____

_____

CHAPTER 8

Understand That Change Is a Process

Slow down. Calm down. Don't worry. Don't hurry. Trust the process.

Alexandra Stoddard[11]

Understanding that change is a process—often a lengthy one—is vital to navigating life's transitions successfully. As you go through change, I suggest that you think less about how long the process takes and more about what the end result will be. This, of course, requires trusting God and believing that allowing the process to unfold in His timing will be worth the wait.

Change can be frightening because we like to be in control, and when things are changing, we don't always know what will happen next and when it will happen. Change occurs because we confront fear, not because we don't feel it. Confronting our fears takes courage—and courage is not the absence of fear but the mastery of it.

> *Courage is not the absence of fear but the mastery of it.*

When we walk with God, change tends to happen in degrees. If we have a goal, we reach it through various levels of opportunity or promotion. We are faithful to one thing for a period, then God gives us more to be responsible for. After we are faithful to that for a while, He will give us more again. We never know how long each phase will take, but we can trust that God knows what He is doing. We usually think we are ready for new opportunities or promotions before we are. Many times, because we think more highly of ourselves than we should, we get frustrated waiting on God as He works in our lives.

Change Often Begins When a Brook Runs Dry

When it's time for something new in our lives, the process of change often begins when we sense what I refer to as "the brook running dry." When we notice this happening, we should pay attention so we don't resist the changes God is trying to bring to us. Let me explain.

The Old Testament prophet Elijah lived during a time of great famine when no water fell on the earth for three years (1 Kings 18:1). God sent him to live by a brook called Cherith, where he drank water and ravens brought him food each day (1 Kings 17:3–6).

> *When one door closes, another one opens if you walk with God.*

Eventually the brook dried up (1 Kings 17:7), and Elijah could no longer count on the daily provisions he had grown accustomed to receiving. But God had another plan, and He always does. When one door closes, another one opens if we are walking with Him. Elijah was told to get up and go to a town called Zarephath, where a widow would provide for him. When he arrived, he asked the widow to give him something to drink and some bread, but she had nothing but a little bit of oil and a handful of meal—only enough to make one last small meal for her son and herself, and then they would die (1 Kings 17:9–12).

Had I been Elijah, this would not have seemed like a promotion to me. Being miraculously fed by a flowing brook with ravens delivering my food sounds better than visiting a poor widow who had given up on life and was predicting her own death.

I share this story to make the point that sometimes, when we must let go of one thing, the next thing may not seem as good. But we need to give it time. Even though Elijah knew the widow had just enough food for herself and her son, he told her to make him something to eat first—before she and her son ate. This was an interesting request because it meant she and her son would have nothing for themselves. Elijah told her that if she would do this, the oil and meal would multiply, and she and her son would have enough until the famine was over (1 Kings 17:13–16).

This was a great test of the widow's faith because, mathematically, it didn't add up. God often works in ways that don't seem to add up from a natural perspective. Sometimes, what He guides us to do seems to make no sense to our minds, yet we feel in our hearts it is what we should do. The widow did prepare something for Elijah to eat, knowing there would be nothing left for her and her son and that they would surely die. But upon her obedience, the oil and meal started to miraculously multiply, and she had enough throughout the entire famine (1 Kings 17:15–16).

Perhaps God didn't send Elijah there for himself but because the widow needed a miracle, and Elijah was good ground to sow into. She prepared a small room for him upstairs in her house, and he stayed there whenever he traveled by that area. First Kings 17:17–22 tells us that her son became ill and died. But Elijah was there, and through a miracle of God, he raised the boy from the dead.

God had Elijah where he needed to be at just the right time. God may place you somewhere for someone else. If you have asked God to use you, don't be surprised if you are sent someplace you would rather not be for a period of time. Your act of obedience may be the open door for your next promotion.

Has Your Brook Run Dry?

Sometimes God wants you to move on to something new.

Think about what you are doing in life right now. Are any of these things no longer fulfilling to you? Do you feel dissatisfied but have no idea why? Sometimes what we are doing is right for a long time, and then for reasons we don't understand, God wants us to move on to something else. One way He helps us to realize this is by withdrawing His grace from what we are doing. In practical terms, this means that what was formerly easy becomes difficult. What was enjoyable becomes a laborious chore. What was satisfying no longer satisfies. What we once liked and enjoyed we begin to dislike immensely.

Dave and I had a young couple living with us in our home for eighteen years, and they took care of our children when we traveled. They also helped run the office in the beginning years of our ministry, and they were valuable beyond anything I can describe.

They had come to work for us when they had been married only six months, so they basically had never had a normal married life because they sacrificed themselves to be available for anything we needed. We enjoyed them and loved them—and we still do today. However, the brook ran dry, so to speak, and we became dissatisfied having people living in our home. During that same season, they began to want something different for themselves. When the time came for them to have a different life and for us to be alone, it took at least a year for all of us to realize why we felt as we did. We had to figure out that it was time for that season of their lives and ours to come to an end.

If you have been doing something for a long time and God calls for a change, it may be confusing to you. I mentioned that when God wanted me to leave my job at the church where I worked and start Joyce Meyer Ministries, I stopped enjoying things and duties I had enjoyed for five years. This was confusing to me. Change is not easy, no matter when it comes, but the longer we have been doing something, the more difficult it is to change it.

> When God calls for a change, it may be confusing to you.

If you are attending a church where you are not being fed spiritually, or if you no longer feel led to serve in any area and you dread going to services, maybe the brook has run dry for you, and God wants to use you somewhere else.

This doesn't mean something is wrong with the church you currently attend; it simply means God has a new plan. Maybe He needs you in a different church.

When the brook runs dry in our lives, we not only feel dissatisfied, discontent, and unhappy, but if we don't make a change, we may start thinking, *What's wrong with me?* Or we will begin to find fault with everything and perhaps everyone around us. We can start placing blame on others, and this can lead to anger and gossip, which leads to strife. God hates strife because it hinders the life flow of His anointing (enabling power).

A woman who attended my meetings for years once told me that she found herself no longer benefitting from them and began to think that perhaps I had sin in my life or was losing my anointing. She prayed for me, and as she did, God showed her that I wasn't the problem. The problem was that she was full from all she had received and wasn't sharing it with others. Because she had no room in her life for anything else, she was no longer receiving anything. She then began coming to the meetings with the idea of ministering to others and started receiving once again.

The brook in your life can run dry in several other areas. Let's look at some of them specifically.

Your Job

Has the brook run dry for you at work? Maybe you need to apply for a promotion, work in a different department, change organizations, or move to a new field. When we have job openings at our office, we post them and give current employees an opportunity to apply for them before looking to hire candidates from outside the ministry. Often a current employee transfers from their department to another one. This is not because anything is wrong where they are; they simply need something new or more challenging.

Eventually, where my job was concerned, the ministry I loved and enjoyed became like a dry brook for me. But I didn't need to leave it. All God wanted was for me to change the way I did things and start delegating more to other people. I had worked hard for a long time, and I needed more rest and free time. In addition, our sons needed to come forward and start forging their destiny. It was time for me to let go of some things I'd always done.

Your Marriage

Has the brook run dry in your marriage? This doesn't mean you need to find a new marriage partner. You and your spouse may simply need some adventure. Maybe the two of you need more personal time together, a vacation, a date night once a week, more conversation, a goal you can work toward together, or any number of other things. Pray about it and let God show you what to do.

Your Behavior

Our own behavior can become a dry brook. We may grow weary of the way we act. That's when it's time to get serious with God and let Him change us. Do you ever get tired of

Do you ever get tired of yourself? yourself? Perhaps you are weary of the way you handle certain situations or of the patterns and routines you have developed. I have gotten tired of myself at times. When this happens, it's often a clear signal that change is necessary. We should be more than ready to let God change us!

Your Friendships

Even a friendship can become a dry brook. Perhaps the friendship is changing, and the season for that relationship is over. For example, you may have become a crutch for another person, and it is time for them to get closer to God than they are to you, or vice versa. Maybe your life is going in a different direction than your friend's life in some area. An example of this would be when one person moves away from the other and begins a new life in a new location; or when one person is busy with young children while the other is happily single and pursuing a career; or when one person needs to care for aging parents and the other does not. In such situations, relationships may need to adjust due to differences in priorities and availability.

Your Commitments

At times, you may have made commitments and been faithful to fulfill them for many years, but you begin to feel it's time to let go. The people involved in these activities will, of course, tell you they don't know what they'll do without you, but we must be Spirit-led, not people-led.

Few situations last a lifetime. Our relationship with God should last forever, a marriage should last as long as both partners live, and our family relationships and perhaps very special friendships may last from the time those relationships are formed until death changes them. But most things have an expiration date, and if we keep them too long, they will get stale.

If your brook has dried up in any way, change something. You may find yourself getting excited again. Just remember that whatever we do, we want to give it our all and do it with zeal and enthusiasm.

> *Things get stale if you keep them past their expiration date.*

Take Time to Adjust

When things change, give yourself time to get used to new people, places, positions, and responsibilities. Don't rush the adjustments you need to make. When I made changes to my job responsibilities, it took time for me to get used to not doing some of the things I had previously done and enjoyed. Sometimes when our missions teams go to India or Africa, I feel a little sad that I can't go. But I know the changes I have made are necessary if I want to be strong to finish the call on my life. For that to happen, I had to make changes.

I wanted less responsibility, but I felt upset and frustrated when decisions were made without me. I finally realized I couldn't have both, and I wanted less responsibility more than I wanted to be involved, so I had to get used to not being involved in everything. Now it doesn't bother me. I have seen that people do just fine without my input.

When Moses died and God called Joshua to take his place, He said, "As I was with Moses, so I will be with you" (Joshua 1:5). Herein lies the key. It isn't who does what that matters as much as whom God anoints to do it. I have watched God move His anointing (His grace, power, and ability to do something) from me to other people for them to do what I have done at times. Since I am no longer anointed to do those things, trying to do them would wear me out. If you have been doing something and you now feel that God is prompting you to delegate it to someone else, I strongly suggest that you do it, because if you keep trying to do something God isn't anointing you for any longer, you will end up hating it, or at least being miserable and worn out.

Starting something is easy, but to finish we must often be willing to make changes along the way. I know I will need to make additional changes as I continue to age. I believe I will always bear good fruit for God's kingdom as long as I

To finish something you must be willing to make changes along the way.

am on earth, but I will have to make changes in order to do so. I already know this, so I'll do what I am doing as long as I can and be ready to change what I need to change.

If you will learn to believe that change is a regular part of life, then when situations or people do change, it won't be so hard on you. View change as positive and expect it to make things better. Don't look at what you are giving up; look at what you'll gain.

Questions

1. How does understanding that change is a process—often a lengthy one—help us navigate the changes we face?

_____

_____

_____

2. What does it mean to say the "brook has run dry" in an area of your life, and how does the story of Elijah help us understand this concept?

_____

_____

_____

3. Has the brook run dry in any of these areas in your life? If so, how can you tell?
   - Your job
   - Your marriage
   - Your behavior

- Your friendships
- Your commitments

_____

_____

_____

4. What is the best thing to do when a brook is running
   dry in some way?

_____

_____

_____

5. Why is it important to take time to adjust to the changes
   that come to your life?

_____

_____

_____

CHAPTER 9

How to Handle the Changes in Your Life

Part 1

For those whom He foreknew [of whom He was aware and loved beforehand], He also destined from the beginning [foreordaining them] to be molded into the image of His Son [and share inwardly His likeness], that He might become the firstborn among many brethren.

Romans 8:29

Often, when something needs to change, we are the only ones who can change it, especially if it is something in our own lives. We should ask for and receive God's help, but we also need to take responsibility to make the changes that need to be made. What do you do when you realize things are not as they should be? Some people get angry, some become depressed or sink into self-pity, some find someone or something to blame, and some are brave enough to try something new. They act on the change they want to see.

When you find yourself in a situation you don't like, you may be tempted to develop a victim mentality. Resist it. If you don't like the way things are going in your life, decide to change what you can change, and pray about the rest of it.

> Change what you can, and pray about what you can't.

In this chapter and the next one, I'd like to share several important lessons I have learned on my journey of changes, and I pray they will help you as you navigate the transitions in your life.

Lesson 1. Keep God First

I had to learn that the most important thing in my relationship with God is to keep Him in first place because this is the place that belongs to Him. In the beginning of our relationship with God, we usually seek Him and ask Him to do things for us, and that is fine. But eventually, He wants us to transition from seeking Him for His blessings to seeking Him for who He is. Instead of always asking God to do something for you, ask Him what you can do for Him. We should seek His face, not just His hand. The Amplified Bible, Classic Edition, indicates that the word *seek* means to "inquire for, and crave peace and pursue (go after) it" (Psalm 34:14).

In Psalm 27:8, David writes, "You have said, Seek My face [inquire for and require My presence as your vital need]. My heart says to You, Your face (Your presence), Lord, will I seek, inquire for, and require [of necessity and on the authority of Your Word]." For David, seeking God's face was a vital need, and we should feel the same way about it. We can do without many things, but we cannot do without God's presence.

The apostle Paul prayed this passionate prayer in Philippians 3:10:

> [For my determined purpose is] that I may know Him [that I may progressively become more deeply and intimately acquainted with Him, perceiving and recognizing and understanding the wonders of His Person more strongly and more clearly], and that I may in that same way come to know the power outflowing from His

resurrection [which it exerts over believers], and that I may so share His sufferings as to be continually transformed [in spirit into His likeness even] to His death.

In simple, practical terms, we can give God first place by putting Him first as we make decisions about how to spend our time. Do your best to begin each day spending time with God, thinking about Him, talking to Him, desiring Him, and putting His will above your own throughout the day. We spend our time on what is most important to us. I have discovered that I can always find time to do the things I really want to do, and I'm sure you do also. We find time to watch television, play sports, go shopping, go out to eat, and pursue other activities we enjoy. Ask yourself what is most important to you. If it isn't God, then make the adjustments you need to make to keep Him in first place in your life.

> *We spend our time on what is most important to us.*

Lesson 2. Know What It Means to Be in Christ

Knowing who we are in Christ is one of the most important spiritual realities we need to understand as believers. We often focus on what we *do* in life but should instead focus on who we *are* in Him. We don't do everything right, but we are always God's children, and He always loves us.

We cannot buy or earn His love or favor with any amount of good works. We should seek to do good things and to behave properly, but we should do this because we love Jesus, not to try to get Him to love us.

For years, I was a workaholic who derived my worth and value from what I did, and I always thought God loved me more when I did good works than when I was enjoying myself or resting. I was deceived and did not know how to receive the gift of right standing with God through my faith in Christ.

I felt good about myself when I performed well, and I felt guilty and condemned when I didn't. I was trying to earn God's love and acceptance through what I did instead of receiving it through what Jesus did. This was one of the most difficult lessons for me to learn in my walk with God. It seemed unbelievable that God could love me for who I was even on days when I didn't do the right things. I was trying to earn what God had freely given, and I needed to learn how to receive freely. The more we learn to receive what God has given us, the more we fall in love with Jesus—and our love is what He wants most. The first and most important commandment is to love God with all of our heart, soul, mind, and strength (Mark 12:28–31).

Knowing we are in right standing with God produces good works, but good works apart from faith will never make us right with Him. Under the Old Covenant, people had to keep the law to be acceptable to God. When they didn't, they had to make sacrifices. But under the New

Covenant, which is sealed with the blood of Jesus, we are made right with God through trusting Jesus' work in His death, burial, and resurrection. Under this covenant, we confess our sins to God, and He forgives us because of our faith and gives us His righteousness. Self-righteousness will never be acceptable to God, but we are fully and unconditionally accepted through receiving and believing in the gift of righteousness provided through Christ's sacrifice.

Lesson 3. Receive and Give Love

The search for self-worth ends in Christ. He loves us, and He proved it when He died for us in spite of our sin (Romans 5:8). We cannot give away what we don't have, so if we want to be able to love others unconditionally, we must first receive God's unconditional love. Read Paul's words about God's love in Ephesians 1:4–5:

> *The search for self-worth ends in Christ.*

Even as [in His love] He chose us [actually picked us out for Himself as His own] in Christ before the foundation of the world, that we should be holy (consecrated and set apart for Him) and blameless in His sight, even above reproach, before Him in love. For He foreordained us (destined us, planned in love for us) to be adopted (revealed) as His own children through Jesus

Christ, in accordance with the purpose of His will [because it pleased Him and was His kind intent].

You can see from this scripture that God loves us because He wants to, not because we deserve His love. In Isaiah 38:17, King Hezekiah praises God for healing him, saying, "You have loved back my life from the pit." For a long time, I lived in a pit of despair, and God's love certainly rescued me. God's love brings us through every problem (Romans 8:25–39). When we are going through difficulties and painful circumstances we don't understand, remembering that God loves us helps us to not give up and to have hope for the future. No matter how unfair a situation seems, we can rest in knowing that God is a just God, and He always makes wrong things right in due time.

The amplification of 1 John 4:16 says we should "understand, recognize" and be "conscious of" God's love. Watching for God's love in my life is one of my favorite things to do, and I encourage you to watch for His love in your life too. God often shows His love for us in little ways as well as big ones, but we miss it because we are not paying attention or we attribute our good fortune to coincidence or luck. Don't give fortune, coincidence, or luck credit for what God does.

Because God loves you, He will give you favor, and you will find people doing things for you for no apparent reason. Receive God's love and think often, *God loves me.* Love yourself because God loves you, and let love flow through you to others.

Jesus gives us a command: to love God (Mark 12:30). He also gives us a second command, which is to love others as we love ourselves (Mark 12:31). If we will focus on these, we will fulfill all of the other commandments.

Lesson 4. Understand Grace

I wore myself out trying to change myself until I came to understand that only God's grace (undeserved favor and power) could change me. One day I was reading the Bible and came across a scripture that has been life-changing for me:

> But He gives us more and more grace (power of the Holy Spirit, to meet this evil tendency and all others fully). That is why He says, God sets Himself against the proud and haughty, but gives grace [continually] to the lowly (those who are humble enough to receive it).
>
> James 4:6

I had been struggling with all my evil tendencies and trying so hard to change myself that I was constantly frustrated. Our willpower cannot change us; only the power of the Holy Spirit can do that. I was "trying" to change, but I wasn't asking God to change me or even to show me what to do. God's grace encompasses more than undeserved favor; it also involves the power of the Holy Spirit, freely given to us, to help us do with ease what we could never do on our own.

Once I learned that only God's grace could change me, I took a different approach to overcoming evil tendencies. Instead of trying in my human strength to overcome them, I admitted them, asked for and received forgiveness, and asked God to change me and show me anything He wanted me to do. Then I waited on Him. I studied what His Word says about the areas in my life that needed to change. I also prayed and confessed the Word—and God basically did the rest.

I'll say it again: *We cannot change ourselves*. Only God can change people. He changes us from the inside out. As part of the process of changing us, He changes our desires.

> Only God can change people.

We wait for Him to act, and then when the change comes, we give Him the credit because we know we didn't do it ourselves.

We want change in ourselves, and Philippians 1:6 says, "And I am convinced and sure of this very thing, that He Who began a good work in you will continue until the day of Jesus Christ [right up to the time of His return], developing [that good work] and perfecting and bringing it to full completion in you." Turn all of your trying into believing, and you will see progress.

Where sin abounds, grace abounds much more (Romans 5:20). God's grace is always available to us, but we must ask for it and receive it. We are saved by grace, and we must learn to live by grace.

Questions

1. What area in your life is changing, or where would you like to see a change? In this situation, what is your part to do, and what is God's part?

_____

_____

_____

2. What can you do to keep God in first place in your life?

_____

_____

_____

3. Who are you in Christ? How does that affect who you *are*—not what you *do*?

_____

_____

_____

4. How can you change your thinking in order to personally receive God's love?

   _____

   _____

   _____

5. Why can only God's grace bring change to a person's
   life? What do you need to stop doing to try to change
   yourself so you can allow God to change you?

   _____

   _____

   _____

CHAPTER 10

How to Handle the Changes in Your Life

Part 2

Every success story is a tale of constant adaption, revision and change.

Richard Branson[12]

One Thanksgiving morning many years ago, I was praying, and I had a vision of a trophy case in heaven full of trophies. God spoke to my heart: "Joyce, you are a trophy of my grace." I had never heard anything like this, but I knew immediately that God was showing me that the work He had done in me added another trophy to His case of transformed lives. A few days later, I saw 2 Corinthians 2:14 for the first time, and it thrilled my heart to have this confirmation of what God had put in my heart. It says, "But thanks be to God, Who in Christ always leads us in triumph [as trophies of Christ's victory] and through us spreads and makes evident the fragrance of the knowledge of God everywhere."

If God can change me, He can change anyone. Anyone—including you—can be a trophy of His grace and power to heal, strengthen, and transform. I have read that the greatest testimony anyone can have is that of a changed life. My life has been changed through God's Word, grace, and power, and the transformation is still in progress.

> The greatest testimony is a changed life.

In the previous chapter, I shared four lessons I have learned about dealing with change. In this chapter, I'd like to share five more of them. I have to remember and practice each of these lessons regularly, and I believe that if you will do the same, you'll also find yourself navigating the changes in your life successfully as you become another trophy of God's grace.

Lesson 5. Be Honest about Yourself and Other People

We cannot be changed into who God wants us to be unless we honestly face our current behavior and attitudes. This is not easy to do, but when we face the truth, we can be set free (John 8:31–32). I recently read that spiritual integrity includes the ability to be brutally honest with oneself. I wasted many years blaming my bad behavior on the abuse in my past and on other people. I used those experiences as excuses to remain the way I was instead of going through the pain of changing. Yes, changing is often painful, but remaining the same and never changing is more painful.

> *You must face where you are in your spiritual growth.*

We cannot move forward unless we squarely face where we are in our spiritual growth. Consider these questions:

- Are you a carnal Christian (one who wants to be a Christian but also wants to live according to the world's ways) or a spiritual Christian (one who is completely surrendered to God and to following Him, even when His ways are different from the world's ways)?

- Are you a baby Christian (one who knows God, but hasn't yet begun to live according to His Word) who has been saved for twenty years but has never grown spiritually?
- Are you a mature Christian who has surrendered your will to God?

I had to ask myself these questions and answer them honestly, and it was hard.

The Old Testament prophet Jeremiah writes that "the heart is deceitful above all things" (Jeremiah 17:9). When something is deceitful, it leads us to believe a lie. For years, I was deceived into believing I was okay and the people around me needed to change. I prayed for Dave to change when we were not getting along. I prayed for my children to change so I could enjoy my life instead of dealing with their bad behavior, and I especially prayed for uncomfortable circumstances in my life to change so I could be happy. After many years of frustration, God finally got me to realize that I was the one who needed to change.

Life will always be full of circumstances we don't like, but the closer we are to God, the less they will bother us. We learn that we can pray, cast our care on God (1 Peter 5:7), and trust Him to do what needs to be done. While we wait and He works on our problems, we can enjoy our lives.

People do things we don't like, but we do things others do not like. God's Word tells us to bear with the failings of the weak and not to live to please ourselves (Romans

15:1). When I think of all the bad behavior Dave and other people put up with from me, I can find no excuse for being unwilling to bear with the faults and weaknesses of others. Instead of trying to change other people and make them what you want them to be, ask God to change you and pray for them to be submitted to God's will, whatever that might be.

Lesson 6. Enjoy Yourself and Your Life

Genesis 1 records God's creation of our universe. Several times throughout the account of the six days of creation, the Bible says, "and God saw that it was good" (Genesis 1:12, 18, 21, 25). At the end of the sixth day of creation, when He was finished, we read, "God saw all that he had made, and it was very good. And there was evening, and there was morning—the sixth day" (Genesis 1:31 NIV).

God took time to *enjoy* everything He created. Based on this, I have learned to take time to pay attention to what God does in me and in my life—and to see that it is good and enjoy it.

Are you working hard to own a nice home but not taking time to enjoy it? Are you working hard to raise your children in godly ways, but not taking time to enjoy them? Sometimes we get so caught up in our work that we forget how important it is to take time to enjoy it and to enjoy life.

I've learned to enjoy myself. I'm not talking about doing things that are enjoyable, but just enjoying who I am because I believe I am a trophy of God's grace. Trophies are given to people who are experts in their field, and God is an expert at taking a totally messed up and broken life and making something beautiful out of it. Deborah Stricklin writes in her book *Trophies of His Grace* that "Each of us is called to be a trophy of God's grace—in the way we live, in the way we love others, and in the way we follow God. Our lives serve as a testament to who He is and what He has done!"[13]

Lesson 7. Take Time to Rest

In Genesis 2:2 we read, "And on the seventh day God ended His work which He had done; and He rested on the seventh day from all His work which He had done."

It is important to work hard, but we also need to remember that we should rest from our work. This doesn't necessarily mean going on a vacation, spending a day at the spa, or taking a nap. It simply means we should not spend all our time working. We need to do things that refresh and restore us. We also need to get adequate sleep each night. If God realized the importance of rest, certainly we can understand that we need to rest too.

Lesson 8. Have Realistic Expectations

Don't expect to love everything about the change immediately. In every change, there are things we will love and things we won't. Dave and I have twin granddaughters who are twenty-one years old. About a year ago, they wanted to move away from home and get an apartment together, and their parents (our daughter and son-in-law) were fine with this idea. As a matter of fact, their parents thought moving out would help the girls take on more responsibility. They love their new freedom, having no curfews, having as much company as they want when they want it, and sleeping as late as they please. But they also have to be more careful with their money now because they have expenses they didn't have before.

There are two sides to every situation. If you get a promotion at work, you'll also most likely have more responsibility. If you get a new car and finance it, you'll also be making payments on it every month for several years. If you get married, you'll experience many wonderful things, but you'll no longer be free to do anything you want to anytime you want to do it. Your spouse may have annoying habits you didn't know they had, or you may face other challenges.

Unrealistic expectations are a big problem for many people. Nothing in life is perfect, and if you expect it to be, you set yourself up for disappointment. Only God is perfect, and only He never changes. He says in Malachi 3:6,

> Only God is perfect, and only He never changes.

"For I am the Lord, I do not change [but remain faithful to My covenant with you]; that is why you, O sons of Jacob, have not come to an end"

(AMP). And Hebrews 13:8 says, "Jesus Christ (the Messiah) is [always] the same, yesterday, today, [yes] and forever (to the ages)."

Lesson 9. Resist Resisting

The last lesson I want to mention—and it is vitally important—is to embrace change when it comes. When we are confronted with change, our first reaction is often to resist, so we need to understand how to resist the tendency to resist. As I mentioned in an earlier chapter, it's important to change your mind about change and view it as a positive, not a negative. It's also important to validate your feelings. It is okay to feel a bit nervous about letting go of the old and heading toward something new. In addition, when facing change, learn to manage your expectations. Don't expect immediate perfection, because change takes time to get accustomed to. Don't expect too much of yourself too soon, and don't compare your reaction to someone else's. It is fine to take it slowly.

Look back at the changes in your life that you initially resisted but brought you to a better place. This will help you realize that whatever is changing now will probably turn out well, too. When things are changing in your life, remember that God is with you and will guide you through anything you have to deal with. Trust Him and continue enjoying life, no matter what.

My own personal transformation from brokenness to

wholeness took quite a while, and initially, I was impatient and in a big hurry for the changes to happen. However, over the years I have learned that staying in God's rhythm is the best way to live. I still practice the lessons I have shared in this chapter and the preceding one. When we walk with God, we never stop growing and changing, so it is important for us to handle each change well.

Questions

1. When we abide in God's Word and honestly face the truth about our behavior and attitudes, what is the result, according to John 8:21–32?

   _____

   _____

   _____

2. What can you do today—even if it's a small thing—to bring enjoyment to your life?

   _____

   _____

   _____

3. Why is it important to rest?

   _____

   _____

   _____

4. What change do you want to make in your life? How can having realistic expectations help you thrive in the process of that change?

_____

_____

_____

5. Think about a change you made that you resisted at first but turned out well. What happened? How does this experience encourage you to make the next change in your life?

_____

_____

_____

CHAPTER 11

Control Your Emotions

You own your feelings. You own your thoughts. You control both. No one has the right to any of it—to any of you without your permission.

Carlos Wallace[14]

Change provokes all kinds of emotions. If a person is typically unstable emotionally, change certainly will ignite all kinds of emotions, and it would be unwise to follow any of them. Even if a person is usually stable emotionally, change can make them moody or more sensitive than usual. We are wise not to make important decisions during emotional highs or lows. I often say, "Let emotions subside and then decide." Emotions fluctuate. We may go to bed feeling one way and wake up feeling differently.

We cannot control when emotions flare up or sink down, but we can learn not to let them control us if we understand the nature of them. I have read that emotions are the believer's number one enemy. People often tell us how they feel when they should be telling us what they believe. Feelings come and go and are unreliable. With God's help we can control our emotions. Even when we feel them, we don't have to vent them. If we don't feel them, we can still do what we need to do, even if we don't have emotions such as excitement or courage to support us.

> People say what they feel instead of what they believe.

Dealing with Toxic Emotions

Emotions can be toxic, meaning that they can affect us—and our health and well-being—in negative ways. Don

Colbert's book *Deadly Emotions* mentions several toxic emotions, including:

- anger
- hostility
- rage
- shame
- guilt
- fear
- worry
- resentment and bitterness[15]

The Bible addresses these emotions and warns of the danger of not dealing with many of them. I don't have room in this book to elaborate on each of them, but I will write about anger and worry, because so many people experience them. Later in the book, you will find an entire chapter on overcoming fear, called "The Courage to Change."

Anger

One of the toxic emotions some people feel when faced with change, especially when they didn't initiate it, when they don't like it, or when it wasn't their idea, is anger. They may become angry because they feel they are losing something, when in reality, they may be gaining something better. Or they may be angry because they feel out of control or for other reasons. God may even test us by allowing a change we did not initiate and we don't like simply to teach us to obey the authority over us with a good attitude. Even when those in authority over us don't consider how their decisions or actions will affect us, God is always thinking of us and what will be good for us. He can take even a bad situation and turn it around for good if we trust Him.

Angry, hostile people release more adrenaline and more hormones that increase blood pressure and heart rate than people who are not angry. Angry people also have elevated cortisol problems, which cause sodium retention, and anger raises triglycerides and cholesterol, all of which predispose a person to heart disease.[16]

Clearly, anger isn't a healthy emotion. Ephesians 4:26–27 says, "When angry, do not sin; do not ever let your wrath (your exasperation, your fury or indignation) last until the sun goes down. Leave no [such] room or foothold for the devil [give no opportunity to him]."

Anger is not a sin if it is justified, but holding on to it is a sin. I have found that the quicker I let go of anger, the easier it is to release it. Don't give it time to take root in your soul. Anger can flare up quickly, but I have found that I can control it through positive self-talk and meditating on scriptures regarding the danger of anger. If we don't vent our anger, it will begin to dissipate. Sometimes it is wise to get away from the situation or person that tempts you to become angry. I know one man who goes for a walk when he feels he is on the verge of letting his emotions take control. You can pray for God's help and His strength to resist the urge to remain angry. It is not wise to repress anger, and the way to avoid that is to talk to God about how you feel. King David did this throughout Psalms. He told God how he felt but followed his expressions of emotion with statements of how much he trusted Him to rescue and help him (Psalm 25, 52, 61, 143).

Some people who become angry frequently say they are just quick-tempered or impatient, or that they have a short fuse. No matter what we call it, the tension and stress of anger may make us sick if it is persistent and frequent. All the dis-ease causes disease. I have read that pent-up emotions that are never dealt with cause such problems as back pain, headaches, digestive problems, bowel problems, skin eruptions, ulcers, high blood pressure, heart disease, muscle aches, autoimmune disorders, fibromyalgia, nervous conditions, and other health problems. The symptoms are real, and we can either medicate them or get to the root of the problem. Usually, if we medicate one symptom, anger causes other ones to appear somewhere else. When we refuse to let go of anger, we create an environment inside of ourselves like a pressure cooker, and sooner or later we will blow up.

I recall a funny story about a woman who was at our house cooking Dave and me a wonderful dinner while we were out. She used the pressure cooker to ensure that the roast she was cooking would be extra tender, but somehow the lid blew off and the roast, juice, grease, and all flew up in the air. Unfortunately, this happened near a ceiling fan above the stove—turned on high. Pieces of roast with trimmings flew all over the kitchen and ruined the ceiling.

When we got home, we found our friend sitting in a corner of the kitchen covered in roast and grease, crying. What happened with the pressure cooker in our kitchen is a great visual example of how anger operates in people.

Society today is full of angry people, some of whom don't even know what they are angry about. I think a lot of their anger stems from knowing that something is wrong in our world. It may also be due to tragic things that have occurred in people's lives. They often become angry with God, and instead of trusting Him to bring justice and doing something positive to turn a situation around for good, they merely complain and grow angrier and angrier, resulting in things like road rage, mass shootings, domestic abuse, and other horrific events. At the very least, it makes it difficult to get along with the angry person.

Anger is dangerous, but it is not the only stressor in our lives; there are plenty of others. Although we cannot avoid all of them, we should avoid the ones we can.

Solomon writes in Ecclesiastes 7:9 that anger lodges in the bosom of a fool, and James writes that anger does not promote the righteousness that God desires (James 1:19–20).

Some people become angry when faced with change, but as you can see from reading this section, learning to control the emotion of anger is very important.

Worry

Another common emotion people feel when things are changing in their lives is worry. They worry about how the change will affect them, their loved ones, their livelihood, the opportunities they hope for, or their social circles. Change typically means dealing with new situations, so it is understandable that uncertainty can cause anxiety.

Worry is a useless emotion. It keeps you busy but gets you nowhere. Worry is not faith, and whatever is not of faith is sin (Romans 14:23); therefore, worry is sin. God hears and answers prayers that are prayed in faith, but prayers are most effective when prayed in faith and trust, not worry. We can be like the centurion who was honest with Jesus and said, "Lord, I believe; help my unbelief" (Mark 9:24 NKJV). We don't always have perfect faith, but we do need to take a serious look at worry and trade it for trust in God.

> Worry may come uninvited, but trusting God is a decision.

Worry often comes uninvited, but trusting God is a decision. David frequently voiced his trust in God throughout Psalms, often writing, "I will put my trust in God." Psalm 56:3 is a good example of this, "Whenever I am afraid, I will trust in You" (NKJV).

Satan is the author of worry. He injects our minds with thoughts about all the bad things that will probably happen. We can worry things into existence if we worry about them long enough, but we also can stop them while they are only thoughts intended to make us miserable and lead us to distrust God.

Anytime I begin to worry, I quickly begin to meditate

on Philippians 4:6: "Do not fret or have any anxiety about anything, but in every circumstance and in everything, by prayer and petition (definite requests), with thanksgiving, continue to make your wants known to God."

Replacing destructive and toxic thoughts with God's thoughts is the best way to get rid of them. When we think positive thoughts, there's no room for negative ones. Hope is the expectation of something good, and we need to fill our minds with hope. Jesus says, "So do not worry or be anxious about tomorrow, for tomorrow will have worries and anxieties of its own" (Matthew 6:34).

One of the most challenging aspects of change is that we often must let go of one thing before God shows us the new things He wants us to do. The time between letting go of the old and discovering the new can certainly cause worry. These times test our faith, and the ultimate benefit of them is that our faith becomes stronger as we walk through them.

Just as God gave the Israelites manna one day at a time, He gives us grace one day at a time. We can look at tomorrow or next month or retirement and feel anxious because we don't know what will happen or what we will do. Perhaps today we don't have the resources for retirement, but when the time comes, God will take care of us if we have been faithful and obedient to Him.

Most parents worry about their children, and I was no different. But it was all in vain because they are all grown now and have provided us with twelve grandchildren. Our adult sons and daughters are all responsible, love God, and are good parents, and I am proud to have them as my children. Some of them went through a few unpleasant phases before they got where they are now, but that's often how people learn. Do your best to raise your children according to God's Word, and trust they will turn out fine.

We can imagine things to worry about. We may imagine that someone is thinking bad thoughts about us when they are not thinking about us at all. We might imagine that someone doesn't like us when they don't know us well enough to have decided whether they do or not. We might imagine we will fail, but we haven't even tried. I believe imagination is a gift from God, but we need to use it to imagine good things, not bad things.

> *Always imagine good things, not bad things.*

Many people would say their biggest worry pertains to finances. God has a simple solution for this in His Word. I summarize Luke 6:38 this way: "Give generously and it will be given back to you multiplied many times over." The Bible is filled with wonderful scriptures about the blessing of giving. You'll read more about giving in the next chapter, but for now let's look here at this passage:

> [Remember] this: he who sows sparingly and grudgingly will also reap sparingly and grudgingly, and he who sows generously [that blessings may come to someone] will also reap generously

and with blessings. Let each one [give] as he
has made up his own mind and purposed in his
heart, not reluctantly or sorrowfully or under
compulsion, for God loves (He takes pleasure
in, prizes above other things, and is unwilling
to abandon or to do without) a cheerful (joyous,
"prompt to do it") giver [whose heart is in his
giving].

2 Corinthians 9:6–7

In the past, Dave and I had some lean years financially,
but we continued to give to the work of God's Kingdom, and
God has never failed to come through for us, even if it was
at the last minute. God is faithful, so I encourage you not
to worry about things that haven't happened. Eventually,
our financial situation changed for the better, and I believe
yours will, too, if you are faithful during the lean times.

Don't Let Your Emotions Work against You

Anger, worry, and other negative emotions don't help us as
we go through changes in our lives; they work against us.
As I mentioned at the beginning of this chapter, change
provokes all kinds of emotions. Our feelings can run wild,
but with God's help, we can control the way we respond
to unhealthy emotions. Negative emotions can complicate
the way we handle change, but we can help ourselves navigate change successfully if we learn to control them.

Questions

1. How can David's example in Psalm 143 help you when you are tempted to be angry with someone?

_____

_____

_____

2. Psalm 56:3 says, "Whenever I am afraid, I will trust in You" (NKJV). What are you afraid of, and how can you demonstrate your trust in God in the midst of it?

_____

_____

_____

3. What toxic or destructive thoughts do you need to replace with God's thoughts?

_____

_____

_____

4. How have your emotions worked against you in the past, and what did you learn from that situation?

_____

_____

_____

CHAPTER 12

Let Go and Let God

*Forget the former things; do not dwell on the past.
See, I am doing a new thing! Now it springs up; do
you not perceive it? I am making a way in the wilderness and streams in the wasteland.*

Isaiah 43:18–19 NIV

You may have heard the advice, "Let go and let God." This is another lesson I have learned on my journey through change. If we stop changing, we stop growing. I encourage you never to be afraid to let go of something outdated, no longer relevant, or out of style. God's timing is very important, and there may be times when something is totally right for us, but then a time comes when God wants us to let go of it and move on to something else. There are, of course, things we should always hold onto, such as the truth of God's Word, integrity, love, kindness, gratitude, and excellence—just to name a few. But sometimes, we seem to hang onto what we should let go of and let go of what we should hang onto. Many situations— even some relationships—in life are intended for a season, and Daniel 2:21 teaches us that God "changes times and seasons" (NIV). Even when we don't like or understand certain changes, when we know that God is orchestrating them, we can trust that He will help us end one season well and move on to enjoy the next one.

Think for a moment about the food in your refrigerator. It has an expiration date—a date at which it will go bad. If you eat it before it expires, it will taste good and you will enjoy it. If you eat it too far past the expiration date, it won't taste good, and it may make you sick. The same principle applies to certain circumstances and seasons of life. As long as we are in God's rhythm and timing, they are good for us. But if we stay in them or try to hold onto them too long, they aren't.

We should let go of things when we realize they are not best for us and make the changes that need to be made to guarantee a better future. They say insanity is to keep doing the same thing over and over expecting a different result. Let's not be guilty of this, but be willing to let go and let God show us the next great thing He has for us. Let's let go of everything that holds us back from God's best for us and let God bring about the changes He knows we need in our lives.

Let Go of Things That Stress Your Schedule

Years ago, I reached a point where I was very unhappy about my schedule and frequently found myself complaining about it. Do you know that complaining without taking action never changes anything? God showed me that I made my schedule and that if I didn't like it, I could change it. Millions of people complain about all they must do, but they are the ones who have said yes to everything on their list. Some things in life we must do, but there are others we choose to do, even though they are not vital.

> *Complaining without taking action never changes anything.*

If you feel overloaded, I recommend that you sit down with a piece of paper and write down everything you are doing. Then cross out the things that are not bearing any good fruit in your life and stop doing them. Let them go. Let someone else fulfill those responsibilities, and let God lead you to do only what He would have you do. Your schedule will open immediately, and you will have time to breathe, think, rest, sleep, and enjoy life. Of course, the people who want you to do the things you choose to discontinue may not like it when you stop, but sooner or later in life you will have to decide who you are living for. I can guarantee you that if you are living for God and following His guidance, He will never give you more to do than you can do peacefully.

The simple exercise of letting go of certain items on your to-do list is an easy way to bring positive changes into your life, and you'll quickly feel its impact in your life. I am thankful to have learned to do this, and it has helped me greatly. For many years, I had a false sense of responsibility, and it caused me to take on many things that should have been done by someone else. I also tend to be a rescuer, so I have to be careful about rushing ahead and trying to rescue everyone from their problems because that may not be what God wants me to do.

Forgive

As we allow God to lead us through the changes He wants us to make in our lives, I think the most important thing for us to let go of is any form of offense or unforgiveness we feel toward anyone.

I do believe forgiveness is essential to change, and this is where many people get derailed. They refuse to forgive because they think it isn't fair or they feel that the people who hurt them don't deserve it. Perhaps they don't deserve it, but when we forgive, we do ourselves a favor, not the people who hurt us. We set ourselves free, and even if those who hurt us don't deserve forgiveness, we deserve peace.

Forgiving people who have hurt, wronged, or offended us isn't easy, but it sets us free. In contrast, holding on to unforgiveness is destructive. It steals your peace and is a toxic emotion that can make us sick. I think I can safely say that keeping our hearts free of unforgiveness is one of the most important things we need to do. God's Word tells us over and over that we need to forgive others as He has forgiven us. Ephesians 4:31–32 says, "Let all bitterness and wrath and anger and clamor and slander be put away from you, along with all malice. Be kind to one another, tender-hearted, forgiving one another, as God in Christ forgave you" (ESV).

In addition to being obedient to God, there are two other good reasons to forgive people who hurt us. The first is that if we don't, our prayers cannot be answered. Jesus says that "when you stand praying, if you hold any-thing against anyone, forgive them, so that your Father in heaven may forgive you your sins" (Mark 11:25–26 NIV).

The second is that if we don't forgive, we give Satan an advantage over us (2 Corinthians 2:10–11). Our unwillingness to forgive opens a door that gives him access to our lives. I believe most of the ground the enemy gains in the believer's life comes through unforgiveness. It is amazing how many Christians are angry with someone else. We try to justify our anger, but there is no justification for it because God tells us to forgive and to keep on forgiving (Matthew 18:21–22). If we are willing to obey Him, He will give us the grace we need to do it. As the saying goes, "people who are hurting hurt people," and it is much better to forgive them and pray for them than to stay bitter and destroy your own happiness.

> If you don't forgive, you give Satan an advantage over you.

Unforgiveness doesn't do anyone any good. If you are holding on to pain, hurt, or offense, choose today to let it go. Let God heal you, and let Him deal with the other person.

Give

Do you remember the story of Elijah and the widow? I mentioned it in chapter 8, and pointed out that Elijah asked the widow to prepare a meal for him, knowing that she only had enough oil and flour to cook for herself and her son. This tested her faith, but in the end, it led to a miracle. As a result of her faith, God provided for her and her son until the famine was over (1 Kings 17:12–16).

I view the story of Elijah and the widow as an example

of giving our firstfruits (the first produce or products of our work, or our income) to God and watching Him give back to us multiplied many times over. Teaching on giving isn't very popular these days, but I am grateful that someone taught me to give and to do so generously because it has changed my heart and my bank account. I began giving even when I needed things for myself or my family, but forty-seven years later, I can give to many others and still have enough left for my family and some savings for the future.

Giving is an important way of letting go of something that is important to us and letting God give us back more than we sacrificed. When we let go of some resource or possession we have, we give God an opportunity to bless us or even to do a miracle in our lives. We don't have to think only in terms of giving money. We can also give our time, our gifts and abilities, our encouragement and support, or something as simple as a smile or a compliment.

When we think of giving financially, we can begin with what the Bible teaches about tithing in Malachi 3:10–11. According to this passage, we are to give the first 10 percent of all our increase to God, and He will open the windows of heaven and pour out blessings on those who do. Some people say tithing is now obsolete because it is part of the Old Testament law and therefore not relevant today under the New Covenant. I simply say that if the people could tithe 10 percent under the law, how much more should we do now that we are living under grace? Paul simply tells us to give generously when he writes about being

"liberal and generous of heart, ready to share [with others]"
(1 Timothy 6:18).

Giving has nothing to do with salvation. If you choose
not to give, you don't lose your salvation, but you will miss
blessings and a great deal of the joy that comes from being
generous to others.

When the widow gave Elijah a portion of what was to be
her last meal, she not only set herself up to be fed miraculously throughout the famine, but she became a friend of
Elijah's. Because of that relationship, her son was raised
from the dead (1 Kings 17:17–24).

God gave His only Son to save us from our sins (John
3:16). Surely, we can give generously to see the gospel
preached and to help the poor and needy of this world.
According to Scripture, we reap according to what we sow
(Galatians 6:7).

Jesus says that if we give, it will be given back to us
"good measure, pressed down, shaken together, and running over" (Luke 6:38). In Philippians 4:19, Paul writes to
those who supported his ministry, "And my God will lib-
erally supply (fill to the full) your every need according to
His riches in glory in Christ Jesus." I believe this promise
is just as much for you and me as it was for the believers in
Paul's day.

Giving is important in the process of
change because it teaches us the principle of letting go and watching what
God does as a result.

> Giving teaches
> you how to let go
> and watch what
> God can do.

Questions

1. When has something been totally right for you in one
   season of your life but not right in the next season?
   What did you learn from having to let it go?

   _____

   _____

   _____

2. What are the things that are stressing your schedule
   right now, and what changes do you need to make to get
   more peace in your life?

   _____

   _____

   _____

3. Have you forgiven the people who have hurt, wronged,
   or offended you? Why is forgiveness essential to change?

   _____

   _____

   _____

4. Are you giving to God and to others? Why is giving
   important, and how has God blessed you as a result of
   your giving?

   _____

   _____

   _____

PART 4

Let Change Move You Forward

CHAPTER 13

Perfection Is Impossible

We shall never be clothed with the righteousness of Christ except we first know assuredly that we have no righteousness of our own.

John Calvin[17]

Some people say, "It's hard to live the Christian life." I say, it's not hard; it is impossible. We cannot live it in our own strength, but Christ lives it through us (Galatians 2:20). We must rely on Him entirely and praise Him for every victory we have. Here's a good example. When we are born again, we receive the righteousness of God in Christ. Second Corinthians 5:21 says:

> *Living a Christian life is not hard; it's impossible.*

> For our sake He made Christ [virtually] to be sin Who knew no sin, so that in and through Him we might become [endued with, viewed as being in, and examples of] the righteousness of God [what we ought to be, approved and acceptable and in right relationship with Him, by His goodness].

We are made right with God by placing our faith in Jesus Christ, not by behaving perfectly. This is true for everyone who believes, no matter who we are. Romans 3:23–24 says:

> Since all have sinned and are falling short of the honor and glory which God bestows and receives. [All] are justified and made upright and in right standing with God, freely and

gratuitously by His grace (His unmerited favor
and mercy), through the redemption which is
[provided] in Christ Jesus.

God's Word tells us we are right with God through our
faith in Jesus Christ, but unless we believe it, we will not
experience it. As a young believer, this was one of the most
difficult spiritual truths for me to believe, and my mind
needed to be renewed in this area. I could not believe I was
right with God unless I did everything right—and that
never happens as long as we live in fleshly bodies. Based
on 2 Corinthians 5:21, I probably said "I am the righteousness of God in Christ" a million times before it finally
started to sink in and become a reality to me.

Now, I know that being right with God does not depend
on my doing everything right, but on the fact that Jesus
did everything right for me. Believing this truth has
brought me into the rest and peace of God and enabled me
to enjoy myself while I was changing instead of rejecting
myself because of my imperfections. My heart's desire is
to do everything perfectly, but my
flesh is still catching up with my
heart. You can have a perfect heart
toward God and yet never attain a
perfect performance as long as you
are in a fleshly body.

> You can be right with
> God because Jesus
> does everything
> right for you.

First Samuel 16:7 says, "For God does not see as man
sees, since man looks at the outward appearance, but the

Lord looks at the heart" (NASB). This truth took a long time for me to believe because I spent much of my life feeling guilty. For years, I thought that, somehow, the fact that my father sexually abused me was my fault. I felt guilty all the time, and it was tormenting. It is a wonderful freedom for me to no longer feel that something is wrong with me but to truly believe that I am right with God through Jesus Christ. If you do not already know this powerful truth, it is just as valid for you as it is for me, and believing it will help you relax and enjoy your life while you go through changes.

Sadly, many Christians suffer from the feeling that they never do enough, no matter how much they do. We may feel we don't pray enough, or we don't pray right, or we don't study the Bible enough, or we don't do enough good works. We are correct about this; we can never *do* enough right to make up for the wrong we have done. That's why Jesus came—to do it for us. Satan stays busy reminding us of our failings and shortcomings. But God tells us that we are made right with Him through faith in Christ, that He loves us unconditionally, and that we are precious in His sight and made in His image.

Change Your Spiritual Clothes

Second Corinthians 5:21 helps us understand what Jesus has done for us: "God made him who had no sin to be sin for us, so that in him we might become the righteousness of God" (NIV). Because of this, we can change our spiritual clothes. Let me explain by calling your attention to Ephesians 4:22–24:

> Strip yourselves of your former nature [put off and discard your old unrenewed self] which characterized your previous manner of life and becomes corrupt through lusts and desires that spring from delusion; and be constantly renewed in the spirit of your mind [having a fresh mental and spiritual attitude], and put on the new nature (the regenerate self) created in God's image, [Godlike] in true righteousness and holiness.

This passage instructs us to *put off* the old nature, meaning the person we were on the inside before we received Christ as Lord and Savior (Ephesians 4:22). We're also instructed to *put on* the new nature (Ephesians 4:24). In between these instructions, Ephesians 4:23 tells us to be "constantly renewed in the spirit" of our mind, "having a fresh mental and spiritual attitude." This tells us how to begin to behave as God wants us to. We must learn to think as He thinks, and we learn from His Word what He thinks. The more we allow His Word to teach us how to think, the more we will act as He would have us act.

Remember, we are to put on the new nature. This is a major change that takes place in our lives when we choose to follow Christ. Spiritually speaking, this means we are to clothe ourselves intentionally with the nature Christ has given us. The fact that we put it on doesn't mean we are instantly mature in it. It simply means we are growing in it, and we will be growing for the rest of our lives.

Just imagine a father giving his overcoat to his three-year-old son. The boy puts it on, but of course it's way too big for him. As he grows, the boy wants very much to wear it. Each year he tries it on, and it fits a little bit better. But it won't fit him properly until he is fully grown.

This analogy helps us understand what God gives us in Christ. He gives us righteousness, but it is too big for us until we grow into spiritual maturity. He gives us love and all the fruit of the Holy Spirit (Galatians 5:22–23), but they are too big for us until we grow into spiritual maturity. Everything He gives us fits us better as we grow. All we need to do is know that it is ours and keep growing into the image of Christ. This frees us from the pressure of feeling that we must do everything perfectly and never make mistakes. If we allow ourselves to carry a burden of guilt, it weakens us spiritually and we easily fall back into the same sin for which we have repented.

Your attitude belongs to you, and nobody can make you have a bad one if you don't want to. Your attitude is the mental posture you take toward the events in your life. Have a good attitude toward change, and you will find it much easier to navigate.

Christ Is in You and You Are in Christ

Paul writes in Colossians 1:27, "To them God has chosen to make known among the Gentiles the glorious riches of this mystery, which is *Christ in you,* the hope of glory" (NIV, emphasis mine). This means that when we receive Christ as Lord and Savior, He comes to dwell in us. We become the home of God. Along these lines, Paul also writes:

> Do you not know that your body is the temple (the very sanctuary) of the Holy Spirit Who lives within you, Whom you have received [as a Gift] from God? You are not your own, you were bought with a price [purchased with a preciousness and paid for, made His own]. So then, honor God and bring glory to Him in your body.
>
> 1 Corinthians 6:19–20

It is awe-inspiring to meditate on the fact that God lives in us and is never more than one thought away from us. This knowledge is especially helpful when we find ourselves in the midst of change and uncertainty. I encourage you to invite Him to be part of everything you do and to talk with Him throughout the day about anything and everything. His strength is in you, enabling you to do whatever you need to do

> God is never more than one thought away from you.

(Philippians 4:13). You do not need to live in fear, because God will never allow more to come on you than you can bear (1 Corinthians 10:13).

Just as Christ is in you, you are also in Him. He is the head, and you are part of His body (1 Corinthians 12:27). The body takes its orders from the head, just as we should take our direction from God. Colossians 1:18 says, "He also is the Head of [His] body, the church; seeing He is the Beginning, the Firstborn from among the dead, so that He alone in everything and in every respect might occupy the chief place [stand first and be preeminent]."

One of the most important lessons to learn is that God sees us "in Christ," if we are believers in Him. Many scriptures teach us that we are in Him. This is our new identity, and it is vital for us to learn to accept it. Ephesians 1:7 is just one of many scriptures about our position in Christ. "*In him* we have redemption through his blood, the forgiveness of our trespasses, according to the riches of his grace" (ESV, emphasis mine). The Bible contains many Scripture verses that teach us about what it means to be in Christ. These include:

> For in Him we live and move and have our being.
>
> Acts 17:28

> Therefore if any person is [ingrafted] in Christ (the Messiah) he is a new creation (a new creature altogether); the old [previous moral and spiritual

condition] has passed away. Behold, the fresh and
new has come!

2 Corinthians 5:17

For He made Him who knew no sin to be sin for
us, that we might become the righteousness of
God in Him.

2 Corinthians 5:21 NKJV

Blessed and worthy of praise be the God and
Father of our Lord Jesus Christ, who has blessed
us with every spiritual blessing in the heavenly
realms in Christ.

Ephesians 1:3 AMP

[So that we might be] to the praise and the com-
mendation of His glorious grace (favor and mercy),
which He so freely bestowed on us in the Beloved.

Ephesians 1:6

For we are God's handiwork, created in Christ
Jesus to do good works, which God prepared in
advance for us to do.

Ephesians 2:10 NIV

After receiving God's gift of salvation, the biggest change
you can experience is learning who you are in Christ. This
is a great and wonderful change that is available to all who

will believe, and it makes all other changes easier to navigate than they would be if we did not know how to walk with God and allow His Spirit to lead us and empower us to deal with them. I have said many times that my worst day with Jesus is better than my best day without Him, and I believe this applies to any change you or I may face. Some changes are easy, but when we go through the ones that seem difficult, we're much better off with God than without Him. Because Christ is in us and we are in Him, we can relax and enjoy the journey God takes us on through life. We don't have to do everything right; we can simply rest in Him and trust Him to lead us. Experience has taught me that the more I trust God, the easier life becomes.

> The more you trust God, the easier life becomes.

Questions

1. Why is it impossible to live the Christian life? What makes it possible?

_____

_____

_____

2. What does it mean to change your spiritual clothes, and how does Jesus enable us to do this?

_____

_____

_____

3. When you change your spiritual clothes, what are you
   to put off and what are you to put on?

   _____

   _____

   _____

4. In your own words, what does it mean for you to be in
   Christ and for Christ to be in you?

   _____

   _____

   _____

CHAPTER 14

Possessing Your Inheritance

And if we are [His] children, then we are [His] heirs also: heirs of God and fellow heirs with Christ [sharing His inheritance with Him]; only we must share His suffering if we are to share His glory.

Romans 8:17

What does it mean to be "fellow heirs with Christ"? Christ's inheritance, I believe, is the whole universe, all that is in existence. Hebrews 1:2 says, "But in these last days he has spoken to us by his Son, whom he appointed heir of all things, and through whom also he made the universe" (NIV). I find this hard to process mentally, and perhaps you do too. Everything God has made that is good belongs to us as believers in Christ. Some of it we may possess here on earth, and some of it is reserved, waiting for us in eternity.

Romans 8:17 says we must share Christ's sufferings if we are to share His glory. I'd like to explain the suffering part first, so you don't shrink back and fail to go all the way through to the fullness of His promise.

Obedience is a key to possessing the inheritance that is laid up for us. God has set the table, but He won't make us eat. We may suffer in the flesh when we choose to obey God, because doing so usually means saying no to ourselves. It is hard for us when we don't get what we want, but as we die to self, it gets easier because we learn that God's ways are always better than ours.

We inherit God's promises through faith and patience (Hebrews 6:12), and we all know that being patient comes with a certain amount of suffering. We don't like it, but there is nothing we can do about it but wait and trust that

God's timing is perfect. Of course, we can choose to run away from it, but if we do, then we will stay in bondage.

The devil is our enemy. He roams about "like a lion roaring [in fierce hunger], seeking someone to seize upon and devour" (1 Peter 5:8), and we are to resist him steadfastly in faith (James 4:7). He makes sure that we do not inherit our inheritance without opposition.

To understand this better, let's go back to the story of Moses leading the Israelites out of bondage in Egypt across the wilderness toward the Promised Land. They had been promised portions of the land of Canaan that would become theirs, and it was a land filled with milk, honey, and all good things (Exodus 3:8).

In Old Testament times, owning land was one of the most desired earthly blessings. The Israelites had worked the Egyptians' land as slaves and shared in only some of the harvest, but they wanted their own land to work and harvest. God gave them their own land, which they eventually entered into. The distribution of the land is recorded in Joshua 13–21.

When the Israelites left Egypt, they traveled to Mount Sinai and spent a year there receiving the law (Numbers 1:1). Then they headed to Kadesh Barnea to enter the Promised Land. Moses sent twelve spies to look at the land and to report back to him (Numbers 13). God already knew it was good, but He wanted them to be encouraged and emboldened to go in and take the land. When they went in, they found the fruit to be so abundant that they had to carry clusters of grapes on poles held on the shoulders of two men (v. 23). But in addition to that, they also saw giants (v. 28), and ten of the twelve spies thought the Israelites could not defeat them (v. 31). They said, "We were in our own sight as grasshoppers, and so we were in their sight" (v. 33). Only two of the spies, Joshua and Caleb, said they were well able to conquer the land.

Because of the Israelites' disbelief and disobedience, they were not allowed to enter the Promised Land, and they wandered in the wilderness for forty years. Numbers 14:22–23 explains why this happened:

> Not one of those who saw my glory and the signs
> I performed in Egypt and in the wilderness but
> who disobeyed me and tested me ten times—not
> one of them will ever see the land I promised on
> oath to their ancestors. No one who has treated
> me with contempt will ever see it. (NIV)

The only ones to enter the land were Joshua, Caleb, and those who had been born in the wilderness.

When they were finally ready to begin to take the land, God told Joshua that every place on which the sole of his foot went, He had given to him (Joshua 1:3). I love the idea that God had given it, but Joshua and the Israelites had to take it. Three times in the first nine verses of Joshua 1, God tells His people not to be afraid but to be strong,

You must take what God gives you.

confident, and courageous because He was with them everywhere they went.

The Israelites had to wander in the wilderness for so many years because they were not walking in faith and obedience to God, and they didn't enter the Promised Land without a fight. They had to overcome many obstacles. I once heard that to *possess* the land, they first had to *dispossess* the occupants already there. Every town they took had people living in it—people who were worshipping false gods—and the Israelites had to go to war with them to take their cities.

What Is Your Promised Land?

Our "promised land" may be receiving Christ, overcoming our past, finding peace, learning to enjoy life, being set free from many things that torment us, such as fear, guilt, shame, jealousy, anxiety, worry, and so on. We might imagine that each of these things is a town in the Promised Land that we must conquer, and conquer we will if we ask God to help us and follow His instructions.

I now enjoy a great deal of freedom, and it has been more than forty years since I started my journey of taking my "promised land." I feel like I have fought many wars, as I'm sure many of you do. But we either fight for our freedom or stay in bondage, and I would rather fight with God by my side than

Better to fight alongside God than do nothing and be miserable.

sit and do nothing but be miserable. When I say fight, I don't mean we are in a constant struggle, but we do have to follow the leading of the Holy Spirit, and that requires action on our part. Also, it often requires determination and refusing to give up.

It is interesting to me how many people Jesus met in the Bible who were either sick or in some other kind of trouble, but they were doing nothing to help themselves, and Jesus' simple instruction was to "get up" (John 5:8) or "Arise" (Mark 5:41; Luke 7:14).

In Isaiah 60:1, God says:

> Arise [from the depression and prostration in which circumstances have kept you—rise to a new life]! Shine (be radiant with the glory of the Lord), for your light has come, and the glory of the Lord has risen upon you!

In Isaiah 61:1–3 God promises favor, healing of the brokenhearted, captives set free, beauty for ashes, the oil of joy for mourning, the garment of praise instead of heaviness, and comfort for all who mourn. These are great promises, but one chapter earlier He says to "Arise [from the depression and prostration in which circumstances have kept you]" (Isaiah 60:1). Do you want healing? Are you ready to get up and do your part?

We usually pray for God to do something for us, and many times He does, but quite often when we pray, God shows us something we need to do. Prayer itself is an action on our part that if not taken, nothing will happen. "Ask and it will be given to you; seek and you will find; knock and the door will be opened to you" (Matthew 7:7 NIV). We must do the asking, seeking, and knocking, and then God will do His part.

Do Something Lest You Do Nothing

I love the story I am about to tell you from 2 Kings 7:3–8 (NIV):

> Now there were four men with leprosy at the entrance of the city gate. They said to each other, "Why stay here until we die? If we say, 'We'll go into the city'—the famine is there, and we will die. And if we stay here, we will die. So let's go over to the camp of the Arameans and surrender. If they spare us, we live; if they kill us, then we die." At dusk they got up and went to the camp of the Arameans. When they reached the edge of the camp, no one was there, for the Lord had caused the Arameans to hear the sound of chariots and horses and a great army, so that they said to one another, "Look, the king of Israel has hired the Hittite and Egyptian kings to attack us!" So they got up and fled in the dusk and abandoned their tents and their horses and donkeys.

They left the camp as it was and ran for their lives. The men who had leprosy reached the edge of the camp, entered one of the tents and ate and drank. Then they took silver, gold and clothes, and went off and hid them. They returned and entered another tent and took some things from it and hid them also.

To me, this story means that because the lepers were willing to try to do something, even though it seemed dangerous, God caused the Arameans to hear an army that wasn't really there, so they ran, leaving the camp and its goods for the lepers. I love the statement they made in the beginning in the King James Version: "Why sit we here until we die?"

The world is full of Christians who should do something lest they do nothing. They are sitting around waiting for God to do everything for them, but He wants to do something through them.

I am not suggesting at all that we form our own plans and just do things that are works of our own flesh. But I am suggesting that we become active in following what we believe to be the leading of the Holy Spirt. He leads and guides us to do things that will help us, but He doesn't do everything for us.

Ephesians 3:20 is a scripture that most people love. When I read that scripture to the people attending one of my conferences, they always cheer. It says:

Now to Him who is able to [carry out His purpose and] do superabundantly more than all that we dare ask or think [infinitely beyond our greatest prayers, hopes, or dreams], according to His power that is at work within us (AMP).

This scripture states that God can do more than we can imagine, far over and above anything we could ask, but He does it according to the power that works in us.

Through Christ, you are capable of much more than you may think you are, because He gives you strength, power, and ability.

> *Through Christ you are capable of much more than you think you are.*

Philippians 4:13 says that we can do all things through Christ, who is our strength. We can act through Him, but we still have to perform the action.

God Told Gideon to Arise

One thing we hear often when circumstances are bad is "Someone needs to do something." But it doesn't occur to us that you or I may be the "someone." Gideon, whose story is found in Judges 6–8, was one of those people.

Gideon was an Israelite who lived in a place called Midian. According to Judges 6:1, the Lord had given the Israelites into the hands of the Midianites because they "did evil in the sight of the Lord," and the Midianites oppressed

them powerfully. Because of their oppression, the Israelites cried out to God. As part of His plan to deliver them
from the Midianites, the Angel of the Lord came to Gideon
and said, "The Lord is with you, you mighty man of [fear-
less] courage" (Judges 6:12). God intended to use Gideon
to deliver the people, but Gideon saw himself as small and
insignificant and did not consider that he might be able
to solve the problem (Judges 6:15). Gideon gave God all
kinds of excuses and finally asked God for several confirmations to prove to him that he was hearing God's voice
accurately (Judges 6:17–22, 36–40).

God needed only one person who would believe that
He was bigger than the problems around him and that He
could work through him. Gideon was that person, and
God told him to arise. Judges 7:9 says, "That same night
the Lord said to Gideon, Arise, go down against their
camp, for I have given it into your hand." God had given
the enemy's camp to Gideon, and all he had to do was arise
and take it. God is never without a plan.

In another Old Testament story, Samuel was mourning
over Saul's failure as king, and God said to him, "How long
will you mourn for Saul, since I have rejected him as king
over Israel? Fill your horn with oil and be on your way; I
am sending you to Jesse of Bethlehem. I have chosen one
of his sons to be king" (1 Samuel 16:1 NIV). That son was
David, who did become king years later. Saul failed, but
God had a plan for His people (Israel), and for David. And
He has a plan for you.

Questions

1. What is the key to possessing our inheritance in Christ?

_____

_____

_____

2. Describe your "promised land."

_____

_____

_____

3. In what situation do you believe God is leading you to "do something lest you do nothing"?

_____

_____

_____

4. Do you believe, like Gideon, that God is bigger than the problems around you? What do you need to do to arise in the midst of them?

_____

_____

_____

5. How does the story of Samuel and David encourage you as you persevere in believing that God has a plan for you?

_____

_____

_____

CHAPTER 15

The Courage to Change

God grant me the serenity to accept the things I cannot change, the courage to change the things I can, and the wisdom to know the difference.

Reinhold Niebuhr[18]

My grandmother had the opening quotation for this chapter, called "The Serenity Prayer," on a plaque in her kitchen. As a little girl, I remember feeling that these words seemed to comfort me whenever I read them. At that time, I was being sexually abused by my father, and every effort I had made to change my situation had failed. So I realized that, for the time being, I had to accept the situation until I was old enough to leave home. I was determined to survive and overcome my circumstances. I believe God gave me that determination.

I had told my mother what was happening to me, and she didn't believe me. Later, she caught my father in the act and simply walked away and refused to deal with it. I had tried talking to an aunt and uncle, but they didn't want to get involved. All these instances were sad, and the people who refused to help me were cowardly, but this quote about accepting what I couldn't change gave me the courage to face what I couldn't change—and the courage to change it as soon as I could, when I turned eighteen.

> Courage is doing what you need to do in spite of your fears.

Courage is not the absence of fear; it is facing fear and doing what you need to do in spite of it. We are all afraid at times. Many of the heroes we read

about in the Bible were afraid, and they faced their fear
and moved ahead in faith.

- Moses was afraid and gave God various excuses for
  why he couldn't lead the Israelites out of Egypt (Exodus 3:11; 4:1, 10, 13).
- Gideon was afraid he couldn't do what God wanted
  him to do (Judges 6:15).
- Jeremiah and Timothy felt intimidated because they
  believed they were too young to be called to the ministry (Jeremiah 1:6–7; 1 Timothy 4:12; 2 Timothy 1:7–8).
- David writes, "What time I am afraid, I will have
  confidence in and put my trust and reliance in You"
  (Psalm 56:3).
- Peter was so afraid that he denied even knowing
  Christ three times (Luke 22:54–62).

As we consider this list, it should comfort us if we feel
afraid, because we are in good company. However, we can
"do it afraid," and that is true victory.

The key to peace is to change what you can change,
accept what you can't change, and have the wisdom to
know the difference. If we cannot
change something, God can, and He
will change it at the right time if we
trust Him to do so. It takes courage
to change things, but it also takes
courage to accept what you cannot

Change what you can, accept what you can't, and have the wisdom to know the difference.

change. This may seem impossible for us, but with God all things are possible (Matthew 19:26).

Sometimes, as people experience the changes associated with aging, they don't want to accept that they are unable to do things they once did. Perhaps they don't want to accept that they are getting older. But there is nothing we can do about aging, so we have to accept it. One thing we can do is take good care of ourselves in our younger years, which will keep us strong in our latter years.

Paul writes that he learned to be content, meaning that he was satisfied to the point that he wasn't "disturbed or disquieted" no matter what state he was in (Philippians 4:11). He may have still wanted change, but he was content as he waited on God. Do you have the courage to wait on God to do what you cannot do and to *enjoy* life while you wait? This is a key to being content.

Partner with God in Your Own Change

We cannot change ourselves, but we can cooperate with the Holy Spirit as He works in us to help transform us into the image of Jesus Christ (2 Corinthians 3:18). We can study God's Word, we can pray, and we can surrender to God when He wants us to let go of something or do something we don't want to do. We can ask for His help daily, and when the Holy Spirit convicts us of sin, we can be quick to repent.

God began a good work in you, and He will bring it to

completion (Philippians 1:6). Even if you don't think or feel that God is working in your life, I can assure you that, through His Spirit, He is.

I'll say it again: We cannot change ourselves in our own strength. Paul writes in Galatians 3:1–3:

> O you poor and silly and thoughtless and unreflecting and senseless Galatians! Who has fascinated or bewitched or cast a spell over you, unto whom—right before your very eyes—Jesus Christ (the Messiah) was openly and graphically set forth and portrayed as crucified? Let me ask you this one question: Did you receive the [Holy] Spirit as the result of obeying the Law and doing its works, or was it by hearing [the message of the Gospel] and believing [it]? [Was it from observing a law of rituals or from a message of faith?] Are you so foolish and so senseless and so silly? Having begun [your new life spiritually] with the [Holy] Spirit, are you now reaching perfection [by dependence] on the flesh?

Years ago, I learned from this passage that I could not change myself, and I began asking God to do it instead. In His own timing and in His way, He has done it and is still doing it daily. We must let go and let God be God in our lives. Letting go means giving up control, and it takes great courage.

Are you able to stop trying to control your adult children and instead turn them over to God? Are you able to stop trying to solve problems you cannot solve and instead turn them over to God? Each time you let go, you gain a little more peace, and peace is one of the most valuable qualities we can have. Works of the flesh always frustrate us, but we can let go of our own ways and wait on God to show Himself strong in our situations.

You Cannot Change People

People can change only if they want to, and if they don't, then even God cannot change them. We certainly cannot do it. Instead of trying to make people change, pray for them to develop a desire to change. Not trying to change the people in our lives who do things we don't like or things that we know are hurting them is possibly one of the most frustrating things we deal with in life. But if we commit our way to the Lord, He will deal with people as we pray for them. Only He can bring change to pass (Psalm 37:5). We must learn to love people the way they are, not the way we want them to be. Loving and accepting them provides a stronger motivation for them to want to change than rejecting them if they don't change.

> Love people the way they are, not the way you want them to be.

When we encounter what we consider to be flaws in people, we often pray for them to change. But do we consider that God may be using those people and their flaws to change us? We must learn to be content, even when everything is not going our way.

In the early years of my marriage to Dave, I tried hard to change him—to mold him into who I wanted him to be— but I finally learned that I was not the potter. God is, and only He can change people. He spoke to Jeremiah:

> The word which came to Jeremiah from the Lord: Arise and go down to the potter's house, and there I will cause you to hear My words. Then I went down to the potter's house, and behold, he was working at the wheel. And the vessel that he was making from clay was spoiled in the hand of the potter; so he made it over, reworking it into another vessel as it seemed good to the potter to make it.
>
> Jeremiah 18:1–4

In many situations, I ultimately discovered that I was the one who needed to change. Although it was frustrating, the fact that Dave didn't change was ultimately what God used to bring change in my life.

For example, Dave loved golf and played frequently. I wanted him to give it up and pay more attention to me, and he refused. Dave did pay plenty of attention to me, but I was controlling and wanted all his free time. Had he quit playing golf because I didn't like it, it would have only fed my controlling nature instead of helping me deal with it. We have been married since 1967, and he still plays golf. Now, I encourage him to go and have fun.

Are you frustrated with someone in your life because they won't do what you want them to do? Are you trying to change them? You are wasting your time and energy. Turn the situation over to God, and instead of trying to change someone else, work with the Holy Spirit and let Him change you as He sees fit.

The World Needs to Change

Many people these days would say the world needs to change. We hear "Be the change that you want to see in the world." When you see problems in society, determine to never be passive about them. Instead, do what you can do to change them. Go into the world and be kind to people. Be a light in dark places. The world is filled with angry people who know something is wrong, but they don't realize what the root of the problem is. Often, it is simply that far too many people don't believe in God, or if they do, they are not fully committed to Him and don't express the fruit of their relationship with Him in their daily lives. We can all be ambassadors for Christ. We are His personal representatives, and He is making His appeal to the world through us (2 Corinthians 5:20).

Psalm 37:1–2 says, "Do not fret because of those who are evil or be envious of those who do wrong; for like the grass they will soon wither" (NIV). The first part of the following verse teaches us what we should be doing: "Trust in the Lord, and do good" (Psalm 37:3 NKJV). I love this scripture. It doesn't simply say to trust God. It adds "and do good." Instead of fretting and being frustrated about the evil in the world, let's take this advice commonly attributed to John Wesley: "Do all the good you can, by all the means you can, in all the ways you can, in all the places you can, at all the times you can, to all the people you can, as long as ever you can."

Where there is injustice in the world, bring justice. Where there is discouragement, bring encouragement. Where there is fear, bring faith. God's Word has the answer to every problem the world has, and we have the Word. Through His power and through the power of the Holy Spirit living in us, we can be a force of positive change in the world.

God sent Elijah at a critical moment in Israel's history. Idol worship had spiritually gutted the nation, and false prophets had settled in the land (1 Kings 16:30–33; 18:18–19). God's altars had been dismantled, and His prophets were in hiding (1 Kings 18:13, 30; 19:10, 14). Behind all of this chaos and immorality were two people: King Ahab and his wife, Jezebel (1 Kings 16:29–32; 18:13, 18–19).

Elijah came from Gilead armed with faith and confidence in God (1 Kings 17:1). It is amazing what one person can do to effect positive change—and that person can be you.

> One person can effect change— and that person can be you.

Elijah was a human being just like you and me, yet he prayed earnestly that it would not rain, and it did not rain on the land for three and a half years (James 5:17). Then he prayed for rain and told Ahab rain was coming when there was no sign of rain in the sky except a cloud the size of a man's hand (1 Kings 18:41–42, 44). The rain did come after Elijah had killed hundreds of Ahab and Jezebel's false prophets (1 Kings 18:40). The people saw God's miracles, and these birthed courage in them (1 Kings 18:39).

The great people we read about in the Bible were just that—people. They were people like you and me. We will never be Elijah, but we can have the spirit of Elijah, meaning that we can be courageous, step out in faith, and do all God leads us to do.

As I alluded to in the story about Gideon, a comment we hear frequently is "They need to do something!" Have you ever stopped to ask who "they" are? I finally did and realized that "they" are you and me. If each of us will do what we can do, God will do all we cannot do. We simply need to make ourselves available to God instead of talking about what everyone else needs to do.

There is no doubt that we are living in difficult times.

The answer is not to be afraid of the future but to face it with courage, asking God what He wants us to do. Certainly, each of us can pray, and we can get up each day and do good. You will come across several people every day who need help, encouragement, courage, or simply a smile. Don't be part of the problem in the world by being negative and doing nothing but rehearsing the problems in your conversations. Instead, be part of the solution. Believe that all things are possible with God (Matthew 19:26), pray for revival, and be full of hope. Expect something good to happen in your life and in the world around you.

It is also important that each of us do our civic duty. We elect our government officials and should do our best to be well informed about the candidates running for office. Don't just vote for people who promise great things; vote for people with a proven record of doing what they have promised to do. Change in our society will require change in our government. Pray that God will lead the right people to run for government offices, people who will work toward making laws that are based on God's principles.

Courage is contagious. If you will be courageous, the people around you will catch courage and become courageous also. Satan is hoping that doesn't happen. His hope is that we will cower in fear, expect more evil and negativity, be passive, and do nothing. Let's disappoint him by actively submitting ourselves to God and resisting the devil, and the devil will flee (James 4:7).

Questions

1. What is your biggest fear? How do you need to demonstrate courage and do what you need to do in spite of it?

_____

_____

_____

2. Which Bible character mentioned in this chapter most inspires you because of their faith in the presence of fear? Why?

_____

_____

_____

3. How can you partner with God in your own change?

_____

_____

_____

4. What is the only reason people will change? Why is it important to understand that you can't change them?

_____

_____

_____

5. In what practical ways can you be a positive force for change in the world?

_____

_____

_____

CONCLUSION

This week has been a week of big changes for me, and I admit some of them were hard. I have had the same doctor for twenty-seven years, and she is moving out of town, so I must find a new one. I tried one and realized that physician wasn't a good fit for me, so I must keep looking.

In addition, for various reasons, we need to change our conference schedule and do more from our television studio instead of traveling to so many cities. This is difficult for me because I prefer doing the conferences in person, and I have been doing them for forty years. When we do something for such a long time, changing it isn't easy. We will still do some conferences, just not as many as we are currently doing. I don't want to let go of some of the in-person events, but I know it is the right thing to do. I can still reach a lot of people with the gospel; I simply need to do it differently. To be successful, we must change when we need to change.

After dealing with the situations I have dealt with this week, I wondered if I wrote this book for myself! Trust me when I say that you are not the only one who deals with change. It comes to all of us, and we can manage it coura-geously, trusting God that the things ahead will be better than the ones we leave behind.

God has many good things for you in your future. Everything you have done so far in life will help you do the next thing better because of the experiences you have had. We learn from experience what to do and what not to do. Jesus went through a lot in His thirty-three years on earth. He trained thirty years for a three-year minis-try that was so powerful it still touches millions of people today. The Bible tells us that "He learned [active, special] obedience through what He suffered and, [His completed experience] making Him perfectly [equipped], He became the Author and Source of eternal salvation to all those who give heed and obey Him" (Hebrews 5:8–9).

Maybe you are going through some difficult times in this season of your life, but they may be equipping you for what God wants you to do in the future. When you come out of the storm you are currently facing, you won't be the same person you were when you went into it. Submit joyfully to God's plan, knowing that even if you don't understand what is happening now, God does. He loves you very much and works all things out for the good of those who love Him and want His will (Romans 8:28).

I pray this book has helped you deal with the changes you are facing and will face in your life and has helped you do so with great courage. Every day is a new beginning and brings with it the possibility of change.

> *If you want to fly, you have to give up what weighs you down.*
>
> Roy T. Bennett[19]

NOTES

2002 by Eugene H. Peterson. Used by permission of Nav-Press. All rights reserved. Represented by Tyndale House Publishers, Inc.

Scripture quotations marked AMP are taken from the Amplified® Bible (AMP). Copyright © 2015 by The Lockman Foundation. Used by permission. www.lockman.org.

1. George Bernard Shaw, *Everybody's Political What's What* (Dodd, Mead, 1944).
2. Alfred Armand Montapert, *Distilled Wisdom* (Englewood Cliffs, NJ: Prentice Hall, 1965), 36.
3. "Transform," in *Cambridge Advanced Learner's Dictionary and Thesaurus* [online] (Cambridge University Press, n.d.), https://dictionary.cambridge.org/us/dictionary/english/transform.
4. "Average Human Attention Span By Age: 31 Statistics," The Treetop ABA Therapy, July 17, 2024, https://www.thetreetop.com/statistics/average-human-attention-span.
5. BrainyQuote, https://www.brainyquote.com/quotes/maya_angelou_101310.
6. Andrew Murray, *Humility* (Whitaker House, 1982), 13.
7. Selena Barrientos and Yaa Bofah, "30 Quotes about Peace That Will Inspire Tranquility in Your Life," *Good Housekeeping*, August 24, 2021, https://www.goodhousekeeping.com/life/a27115824/peace-quotes.
8. Jack LaLanne, *Revitalize Your Life after 50: Improve Your Looks, Your Health, and Your Sex Life* (Hastings House, 1995), 42.
9. Quote Fancy, https://quotefancy.com/quote/953506/Robin-S-Sharma-Don-t-LIVE-the-same-year-75-times-and-call-it-a-Life.
10. John F. Kennedy, speech at Paulskirche, Frankfurt, June 25, 1963.

11. AZ Quotes, https://www.azquotes.com/quote/1497219.

12. Chris Heivly, "Richard Branson's 1 Rule for Embracing Change," *Inc.*, January 14, 2016, https://www.inc.com/chris -heivly/richard-branson-s-one-rule-for-embracing-change .html.

13. Deborah Rae Stricklin, *Trophies of His Grace: Capture the Goodness and Glory of the Grace of God* (Dream Releaser, 2020).

14. Carlos Wallace, *The Other 99 T.Y.M.E.S.: Train Your Mind to Enjoy Serenity* (Million Dollar Pen, Ink, 2016).

15. Don Colbert, *Deadly Emotions: Understand the Mind-Body-Spirit Connection That Can Heal or Destroy You* (Thomas Nelson, 2003), 35.

16. Colbert, *Deadly Emotions*, 37.

17. AZ Quotes, https://www.azquotes.com/quote/927659?ref =righteousness.

18. BrainyQuote, https://www.brainyquote.com/quotes/reinhold _niebuhr_100884.

19. QuoteFancy, https://quotefancy.com/quote/3207073/Roy-T -Bennett-Accept-yourself-love-yourself-and-keep-moving -forward-If-you-want-to-fly.

Do you have a real relationship with Jesus?

God loves you! He created you to be a special, unique, one-of-a-kind indi-
vidual, and He has a specific purpose and plan for your life. And through a
personal relationship with your Creator—God—you can discover a way of
life that will truly satisfy your soul.

No matter who you are, what you've done, or where you are in your life
right now, God's love and grace are greater than your sin—your mistakes.
Jesus willingly gave His life so you can receive forgiveness from God and
have new life in Him. He's just waiting for you to invite Him to be your
Savior and Lord.

If you are ready to commit your life to Jesus and follow Him, all you
have to do is ask Him to forgive your sins and give you a fresh start in the
life you are meant to live. Begin by praying this prayer...

*Lord Jesus, thank You for giving Your life for me and forgiving
me of my sins so I can have a personal relationship with You.
I am sincerely sorry for the mistakes I've made, and I know I
need You to help me live right.*

*Your Word says in Romans 10:9, "If you declare with your
mouth, 'Jesus is Lord,' and believe in your heart that God raised
him from the dead, you will be saved" (NIV). I believe You are the
Son of God and confess You as my Savior and Lord. Take me just
as I am, and work in my heart, making me the person You want
me to be. I want to live for You, Jesus, and I am so grateful that
You are giving me a fresh start in my new life with You today.*

I love You, Jesus!

It's so amazing to know that God loves us so much! He wants to have a
deep, intimate relationship with us that grows every day as we spend time
with Him in prayer and Bible study. And we want to encourage you in your
new life in Christ.

Please visit joycemeyer.org/salvation to request Joyce's book *A New Way
of Living*, which is our gift to you. We also have other free resources online
to help you make progress in pursuing everything God has for you.

Congratulations on your fresh start in your life in Christ! We hope to
hear from you soon.

ABOUT THE AUTHOR

Joyce Meyer is one of the world's leading practical Bible teachers and a *New York Times* bestselling author. Joyce's books have helped millions of people find hope and restoration through Jesus Christ. Joyce's program, *Enjoying Everyday Life*, is broadcast on television, radio, and online to millions worldwide in 112 languages.

Through Joyce Meyer Ministries, Joyce teaches internationally on a number of topics with a particular focus on how the Word of God applies to our everyday lives. Her candid communication style allows her to share openly and practically about her experiences so others can apply what she has learned to their lives.

Joyce has authored more than 150 books, which have been translated into more than 160 languages, and over 41 million of her books have been distributed worldwide. Bestsellers include *Power Thoughts*; *The Confident Woman*; *Look Great, Feel Great*; *Starting Your Day Right*; *Ending Your Day Right*; *Approval Addiction*; *How to Hear from God*; *Beauty for Ashes*; and *Battlefield of the Mind*.

Joyce's passion to help people who are hurting is foundational to the vision of Hand of Hope, the missions arm

of Joyce Meyer Ministries. Each year Hand of Hope provides millions of meals for the hungry and malnourished,
installs freshwater wells in poor and remote areas, provides critical relief after natural disasters, and offers free
medical and dental care to thousands through their hospi-
tals and clinics worldwide. Through Project GRL, women
and children are rescued from human trafficking and provided safe places to receive an education, nutritious meals,
and the love of God.

JOYCE MEYER MINISTRIES

U.S. & FOREIGN OFFICE ADDRESSES

Joyce Meyer Ministries
P.O. Box 655
Fenton, MO 63026
USA
(866) 480-1528

Joyce Meyer Ministries—Canada
P.O. Box 7700
Vancouver, BC V6B 4E2
Canada
(800) 868-1002

Joyce Meyer Ministries—Australia
Locked Bag 77
Mansfield Delivery Centre
Queensland 4122
Australia
+61 7 3349 1200

Joyce Meyer Ministries—England
P.O. Box 8267
Reading RG6 9TX
United Kingdom
+44 1753 831102

Joyce Meyer Ministries—South Africa
Unit EB06, East Block, Tannery Park
23 Belmont Road
Rondebosch, Cape Town, South Africa, 7700
+27 21 701 1056

Joyce Meyer Ministries—Francophonie
Boite Postale 53
29 avenue Maurice Chevalier
77330 Ozoir la Ferriere
France

Joyce Meyer Ministries—Germany
Postfach 761001
22060 Hamburg
Germany
+49 (0)40 / 88 88 4 11 11

Joyce Meyer Ministries—Netherlands
Postbus 55
7000 HB Doetinchem The Netherlands
+31 (0)26 20 22 100

Joyce Meyer Ministries—Russia
P.O. Box 789
Moscow 101000
Russia
+7 (495) 727-14-68

OTHER BOOKS BY JOYCE MEYER

100 Inspirational Quotes
100 Ways to Simplify Your Life
21 Ways to Finding Peace and Happiness
The Answer to Anxiety
Any Minute
Approval Addiction
The Approval Fix
Authentically, Uniquely You*
The Battle Belongs to the Lord
Battlefield of the Mind*
Battlefield of the Mind Bible
Battlefield of the Mind for Kids
Battlefield of the Mind for Teens
Battlefield of the Mind Devotional
Battlefield of the Mind New Testament
Be Anxious for Nothing*
Be Joyful
Beauty for Ashes
Being the Person God Made You to Be
Blessed in the Mess
Change Your Words, Change Your Life
Colossians: A Biblical Study
The Confident Mom
The Confident Woman
The Confident Woman Devotional
Do It Afraid*
Do Yourself a Favor...Forgive
Eat the Cookie...Buy the Shoes
Eight Ways to Keep the Devil under Your Feet
Ending Your Day Right
Enjoying Where You Are on the Way to Where You Are Going
Ephesians: A Biblical Study
The Everyday Life Bible
The Everyday Life Psalms and Proverbs
Filled with the Spirit
Finding God's Will for Your Life
Galatians: A Biblical Study

Good Health, Good Life
Habits of a Godly Woman
*Healing the Soul of a Woman**
Healing the Soul of a Woman Devotional
Hearing from God Each Morning
How to Age without Getting Old
*How to Hear from God**
How to Succeed at Being Yourself
How to Talk with God
I Dare You
*If Not for the Grace of God**
In Pursuit of Peace
In Search of Wisdom
James: A Biblical Study
The Joy of Believing Prayer
The Joy of an Uncluttered Life
Knowing God Intimately
A Leader in the Making
Life in the Word
Living beyond Your Feelings
Living Courageously
Look Great, Feel Great
Love Out Loud
The Love Revolution
Loving People Who Are Hard to Love
Making Good Habits, Breaking Bad Habits
Managing Your Emotions
Making Marriage Work
(previously published as *Help Me—I'm Married!*)
*Me and My Big Mouth!**
*The Mind Connection**
Mornings with God
My Time with God
Never Give Up!
Never Lose Heart
New Day, New You
Overcoming Every Problem
Overload
The Pathway to Success
The Penny

Perfect Love (previously published as *God Is Not Mad at You*)*
Philippians: A Biblical Study
The Power of Being Positive
The Power of Being Thankful
The Power of Determination
The Power of Forgiveness
The Power of Simple Prayer
The Power of Thank You
Power Thoughts
Power Thoughts Devotional
Powerful Thinking
Quiet Times with God Devotional
Reduce Me to Love
The Secret Power of Speaking God's Word
The Secrets of Spiritual Power
The Secret to True Happiness
Seven Things That Steal Your Joy
Start Your New Life Today
Starting Your Day Right
Straight Talk
Teenagers Are People Too!
Trusting God Day by Day
What About Me?
The Word, the Name, the Blood
Woman to Woman
You Can Begin Again
*Your Battles Belong to the Lord**

JOYCE MEYER SPANISH TITLES

Amar a la gente que es muy difícil de amar
(Loving People Who Are Hard to Love)
Auténtica y única (Authentically, Uniquely You)
Belleza en lugar de cenizas (Beauty for Ashes)
Bendicion en el desorden (Blessed in the Mess)
Buena salud, buena vida (Good Health, Good Life)
Cambia tus palabras, cambia tu vida
(Change Your Words, Change Your Life)
El campo de batalla de la mente (Battlefield of the Mind)
Cómo envejecer sin avejentarse (How to Age without Getting Old)

Como formar buenos habitos y romper malos habitos (Making Good
Habits, Breaking Bad Habits)
La conexión de la mente (The Mind Connection)
Dios no está enojado contigo (God Is Not Mad at You)
La dosis de aprobación (The Approval Fix)
Efesios: Comentario bíblico (Ephesians: Biblical Commentary)
Empezando tu día bien (Starting Your Day Right)
Hágalo con miedo (Do It Afraid)
Hazte un favor a ti mismo ... perdona (Do Yourself a Favor ... Forgive)
Madre segura de sí misma (The Confident Mom)
Momentos de quietud con Dios (Quiet Times with God Devotional)
Mujer segura de sí misma (The Confident Woman)
No se afane por nada (Be Anxious for Nothing)
Pensamientos de poder (Power Thoughts)
Sanidad para el alma de una mujer (Healing the Soul of a Woman)
Sanidad para el alma de una mujer, devocionario (Healing the Soul of a
Woman Devotional)
Santiago: Comentario bíblico (James: Biblical Commentary)
Sobrecarga (Overload)*
Sus batallas son del Señor (Your Battles Belong to the Lord)
Termina bien tu día (Ending Your Day Right)
Tienes que atreverte (I Dare You)
Usted puede comenzar de nuevo (You Can Begin Again)
Viva amando su vida (Living a Life You Love)
Viva valientemente (Living Courageously)
Vive por encima de tus sentimientos (Living beyond Your Feelings)

* Study Guide available for this title

Books by Dave Meyer

Life Lines